Success

How Teens Can Create Their Own
Brilliant Future

*(Timeless Principles To Develop Inner Confidence
And Create Authentic Success)*

Damian Bishop

Published By **Chris David**

Damian Bishop

All Rights Reserved

Success: How Teens Can Create Their Own Brilliant Future (Timeless Principles To Develop Inner Confidence And Create Authentic Success)

ISBN 978-1-77485-637-6

All rights reserved. No part of this guidebook shall be reproduced in any form without permission in writing from the publisher except in the case of brief quotations embodied in critical articles or reviews.

Legal & Disclaimer

The information contained in this ebook is not designed to replace or take the place of any form of medicine or professional medical advice. The information in this ebook has been provided for educational & entertainment purposes only.

The information contained in this book has been compiled from sources deemed reliable, and it is accurate to the best of the Author's knowledge; however, the Author cannot guarantee its accuracy and validity and cannot be held liable for any errors or omissions. Changes are periodically made to this book. You must consult your doctor or get professional medical advice before using any of the suggested remedies, techniques, or information in this book.

Upon using the information contained in this book, you agree to hold harmless the Author from and against any damages, costs, and expenses, including any legal fees potentially resulting from the application of any of the information provided by this guide. This disclaimer applies to any damages or injury caused by the use and application, whether directly or indirectly, of any advice or information presented, whether for breach of contract, tort, negligence, personal injury, criminal intent, or under any other cause of action.

You agree to accept all risks of using the information presented inside this book. You need to consult a professional medical practitioner in order to ensure you are both able and healthy enough to participate in this program.

Table of contents

Introduction _____ 1

Chapter 1: How Do You Define Success? _ 4

Chapter 2: The Characteristics Of Highly Successful People _____ 7

Chapter 3: Maintain High Enthusiasm __ 19

Chapter 4: Prepare To Facing Obstacles 25

Chapter 5: The Value Of Creative Thinking _____ 29

Chapter 6: Patterns And Habits For Successful People _____ 31

Chapter 7: Knowing When To Make A Change Is Crucial _____ 37

Introduction

The workplace is very different today. These institutions are not preparing graduate students for the job. Many schools tell their students that they should apply for internships in summer between their junior year and their senior year. Actually? It might sound nice, but the reality is that less experience will make it more difficult for you to get your internship. Communication between academics & career services departments is also almost insufficient. Real employers can help you understand what skills are needed. But, this is not the truth. Here's the result. Intel recently removed 100 universities, along with a very generous tuition repayment plan, from its list. These plans were made because of their internal evaluations that showed that those who had taken these courses didn't earn their degrees to the standard expected. There are increasing numbers online that offer training in important topics for today's workplace. If schools were actually doing their job, such areas wouldn't exist. To navigate successfully in this new economy, you have to be familiar with how it works. These factors are key to your ability to improve your career. This is the workplace's new reality.

Overall, it is important to understand how to deal with a constantly changing environment in order to thrive in today's workplace, your career, and be heard. These improvements are briefly described below. We'll be discussing these improvements as we go through this book.

This book will help you, young workers with high prospects, get a clear direction and make a difference in your business. This book can be used by anyone who needs work. Before we get started, let me leave you with one final thought. While this book focuses primarily on thinking within your company, moving forward, and succeeding, it is important that people are open to exploring new possibilities. You need to be able adapt to changing in an ever-changing market. I will give you the options and motivate you throughout this book. Your job success lies within you, and I am here support and encourage you. Let's get started!

Chapter 1: How Do You Define Success?

Each of our cultural backgrounds, life experiences, and influential figures are unique. This is why each person has a different view of success. Each person has a different idea of what success means. And this idea changes as we go through life. What matters most to you at one moment may not matter at another.

Many of us, particularly in our younger years have a narrowly defined idea of success that is driven by materialistic considerations. We set goals to achieve our financial, lifestyle and retirement goals. Because we are so focused on our financial goals in our professional lives, it is common to forget about the needs of others. At this point, success is more about tangible components than it is intangible. As our priorities shift over time, the definition of success will change. If the value of family time is changing, we may need to stop earning income and give up some income.

One of the ways we might give back to our community is to feel compelled to do so. After that, it's back to the drawing boards. A successful perspective is one that changes with time, rather than something that must be defined.

Is it possible to have a formula that works for all people regardless of their ideas about success? Yes! Happiness is a metric that can be used to judge whether success has been achieved. The person who is traveling along the path of success must periodically evaluate their own state and try to find a place of contentment. If someone is constantly unhappy and stressed on their journey to a certain destination, that's not success. Failure can be motivations that lead to the destruction of someone before they are able to achieve them.

We cannot set unrealistic expectations about success. It is important to understand ourselves and be truthful with ourselves. It's very likely that a person of 5'3" will not be able to make it as a professional player. Can it be done? Although this is possible, there have been very few instances of success. It doesn't matter what, it is essential to be aware of the strength, endurance, and willpower required for any given task.

For success to be defined, one must take the moral highground in order achieve it. Any success that comes from the unfair exploitation or profiting off the labor or product others using methods that violate laws, standards and policies would be illegal. It does not mean that these people are unethical, but there is a real danger of such abuse.

Chapter 2: The Characteristics Of Highly Successful People

Every successful person has a competitive streak. This shows passion for their work. It is an essential trait. It's often discovered early in life when it comes to classroom zeal. Sometimes, the child who can't or won't accept "B" may end up getting it. The same kid that arrives at high school after graduation will be the one who places in a science challenge or writes an award-winning article. Their name is on every contest or challenge. To be able to outperform your competitors, you need to have an insatiable passion about what you're doing. Innovativeness and originality are hallmarks of passion, which gives success many people. Bill Gates, his persistence, and innovation led to Microsoft, Inc., although he was far not the first person to do so.

Successful people know when it's time to move on. Learning from mistakes is part of being successful. Tomorrow will present bigger challenges, more opportunities to make mistakes and success people excel at managing this recurring theme. Failure itself is not the most important thing, but how you react to it can have a greater impact than what happened. Some believe that success is only possible through struggle. However, the evidence of this can be seen in the diverse list of individuals from all walks. Oprah Winfrey. Katy Perry. Jim Carrey. Stephen King. Henry Ford. These are people who were initially flat on their faces but were able to rise from the ashes and continue their success stories. What other skills or qualities might people with failures find a way of overcoming? A different way of responding might be the first thing they have. Failing is not more than a colleague's negative opinion on an investment idea. It's easy to feel resentful or disappointed by someone you value and respect. Others will simply go back to the drawing boards and start all over again. They don't react negatively to rejection and they don't take it personally. This means that they have thick skin, which for some is impossible. However, for others it may be an asset. You can also shift the blame when you fail. This is another ability that helps some people to face failure. People tend to take credit, but they may also attribute failure to the difficulty or timing of a task. They may not change anything but might just get back up and try again when things are easier or more favorable.

Successful people place great emphasis on being better at what they do. Strive for improvement is key when all your rivals are deeply invested in improving their skills. Here, self-criticism is essential. They often have unreasonable standards. They rarely feel satisfied with their achievements, and they aren't often happy. Routine assessment of one's strengths and weakness will enable you to make necessary adjustments to ensure that you are improving. It is wonderful to make improvements that are within the control of people, but it doesn't always work out this way. Take the young leader in a budding entrepreneurship. He arrives at work every morning with his cup of excitement full. But he soon finds that the same two coworkers are arguing about small details because they've resolved to never get along. Your first instinct is to ignore them, and let them deal with their differences. The price of doing so is high. So he enrolls in conflict resolution training to make sure that employees who are bickering don't become destructive at work. Even though it may take away from other tasks to go to training sessions with his subordinates, not allowing him to do so could have worse consequences. This is especially true when someone has command of a large staff. If you want to be a better manager and solve these problems, then it's best to train others. Complacency is another trait of people who know the importance to improvement. It is easy for familiarity to dismiss the necessity of a software upgrade. However, it will prove difficult to implement in an expansion. These types of thinking are not practical, and it is likely to lead to lost opportunity quickly if there is potential for new growth or productivity.

Successes are able to pay close attention to the small details that others don't notice or overlook. Some believe that by focusing on small details, it is possible to avoid more serious issues later. This view that small things add-up is a valid one in certain professional fields. Theatre and dining are just two examples. You must perform tasks in a timely manner to ensure a smooth performance whether you are performing on the theatre stage or the culinary scene. You might need to micromanage and help in small things in order for these situations to work. The good news about this is that the people who are required to do so know what to expect. This may not make it more enjoyable to perform the task, but it will help them to be prepared.

Persistence is vital for success. You will face situations that seem impossible to change, but you can overcome them and, in many cases they must be overcome if you want to keep moving forward. It is important for you to recognize the successes along the way and remind yourself of the perseverance necessary to reach them. The people being mentioned here are those that won't take no for an answers. In their attempt to convince hiring officers to give them a chance, these people sometimes drive them nuts. These are female employees and other minorities workers who won't give up on their contributions to the company's growth or accept less than average compensation. Persistence leads to an initial small change in an individual's life or for a small group. But then, eventually, the change is large and affects a large population. Rosa Parks may initially have only earned her own seat on bus by refusing others', but she gained attention and was able to help others earn theirs.

Is it unusual for someone to experience the same situation? This question can be answered by asking the network. The key to success is networking. They know who the best in their work world and recognize the invaluable value of it. They form and nurture relationships among their peers and with competitors. So networking is a matter of being cautious but also being open to new opportunities. Networking is multi-faceted. Networking isn't limited to those in their particular profession. They include alumni associations, young professionals, or other groups that could be of benefit to them. People who have built a strong network come prepared. They're dressed well and have a businesscard that they can pass along to anyone they might like to meet again. They realize that it is impossible to talk or interact with everyone at every conference and meeting. They choose the people most in line with their interests and make an effort to have a conversation with them. Even if they only get an introduction at first, they might extend a businesscard to promote future conversations that may or not take place at their meeting location. They know the importance to the old saying that "you only get one shot at making a lasting impression". Focused attention and eye contact are crucial, but you should take care not to occupy too much of their time.

A successful person must learn how to detach. You will need to be away from your work and recharge. Although the drive to succeed is never ending, professional people must be able recognize when to stop. Professionals need a break. This is if they can't control their egos, self esteem, and drive to get the organization recognized. And sometimes it isn't a constructive-but-challenging component to a coworker's personality that necessitates withdrawal - the person might be downright toxic, at least to the person contemplating a getaway. Many people who succeed are simply burned out. They must face this issue on multiple levels if they are passionate about their job. No matter what motivating factors they may have, every person approaches this key component of success in a different way. If you are suffering from burnout, it is important to establish cut-offs for yourself or others that will allow you to regain your enthusiasm. You might consider starting a new fitness program at your gym to relieve stress temporarily but more often. Some people may require a complete change of scenery. It might be volunteering for charity or a spontaneous trip for someone else.

All successful people must manage chaos and crisis. Everyone will have a personal problem. Individuals with different personalities may present a challenge to supervisors. In either case, there are situations that could prove to be dangerous and need to be overcome. Unexpected crises, or chaotic situations, are by nature situations in which the affected party has little control. You must approach them constructively in order to get the best possible outcome. People who succeed often face similar situations as everyone else. How they approach them and perceive them is what will make the difference. They accept the fact that circumstances are beyond their control. They evaluate the situation to determine what factors or components may be positively affected to change the outcome. Knowing the difference between things that someone can or cannot control is crucial.

Although personality traits and personal tendencies are flexible among successful people, they should be clearly defined. The most predictable people are those who have succeeded. Even though they might not always agree on the same points, successful people will know their reasoning and be able communicate it to others. Transparency is essential in any situation and successful people will openly share this information when needed. High-achieving people might not be as tolerant of their personality quirks than others. There is an aspect to everyone that should be taken into consideration when dealing with them at high stakes. These successful people are similar to others except that they know how to temper their vulnerabilities in high-stakes situations.

Every successful person learns to advocate for those who make a difference and to give back. Giving thanks will reap huge benefits and increase the confidence of clients or colleagues. As their support is crucial for future and continued success, it will take a certain amount of loyalty from both. Some might question the timing. Others would insist that only successful people can make a commitment to giving back. Many philanthropists adopt this approach, while others choose to give even before they are famous or have instant celebrity status. People who adopt the latter approach are said to be able to enjoy an appetizer much before they have to eat a full meal. The modern age is one in which successful people are giving back before they even arrive. This gives them the opportunity to enjoy an appetizer long before any big meal.

Chapter 3: Maintain High Enthusiasm

"Nothing great has ever been achieved without passion." Ralph Waldo Emerson's well-known quote doesn't say it all but it certainly conveys a lot. Enthusiasm wields great power. It is essential that successful people are able to enjoy what they do. Some tasks may not be thrilling but enthusiasm will enable someone to get up every now and again to accomplish what they need to. Most importantly, it gives you strength to face difficult situations or confront adversarial situations. Everyone will encounter obstacles. Enthusiasm makes it possible to make lemonade in such situations. One can make many generalizations about enthusiasm.

To find lasting joy, one must follow the path of their bliss. Prioritize the pursuits that are most meaningful to you. There are more profitable ventures out there, but if a business like owning a kayak outfitter is something you love and has been for a while, invest in it. There will always be another business that makes more money or generates more income. However, the long-term potential benefits of taking on an exciting professional challenge might far outweigh the short term gains.

You can't keep your enthusiasm up when you are constantly experiencing negativity. Find ways to make the best of negative situations and use them as life lessons. Consider yourself a creator when faced with adversity and not a victim. It's easy not to be happy and it is easy sometimes to get discouraged. It is a natural reaction to poor circumstances. But it can also be a temporary one that people may have. If one desires to remain enthusiastic, this cannot be held on to. If you feel that subordinates are creating negativity in your life, be clear and give them a warning. If it doesn't stop, then let them go. A bad assistant can make it difficult for your canoe-outfitter business to succeed. They will cause potential clients to move on and may even be dissatisfied with you.

The two are interconnected in a constant way: enthusiasm and creativity. One cannot exist without another. Innovation and original thinking are the keys to launching enthusiasm into outer space. If a person surrounds themselves with people who are willing to try new things and solve problems, success is likely to be greater. Good observational skills are a key ingredient in creativity. Sometimes, all it takes to increase productivity is a simple improvement in efficiency. You don't need to reinvent everything when minor changes are all that is needed.

Being proactive is always a way to inspire enthusiasm. An active approach encourages others to help promote something they have worked hard on. This gives the initiativer a boost and also helps to gain respect from others. If you want to win the confidence of your peers or others within your network of influence, there's no better way than to jump in the first chance.

To keep enthusiasm from suffocating, it is necessary to be rational. In order to achieve a success outcome, logic must be used at all times. Realistic expectations are impossible to meet, regardless of how much energy you have or how much excitement. High-achieving people are enthusiastic and have the patience to endure the difficult process. Most successful endeavors can't be finished immediately after they are started. Things happen slowly and people need to do the right thing to ensure that they happen. People need to realize that their enthusiasm should not lead to impatience. It is possible that someone who opens a new vegetable farm will expect to see the first yields be similar to those of subsequent years. This is because there will likely still be learning curves in many areas. Sometimes, it will be necessary to modify the soil and apply herbicides or other chemicals. This may require some trial-and–error. If you want to achieve success in this endeavor, it is best to learn as you go.

Patience is an alternative for unbridled excitement. To give enthusiasm some space, patience is a good alternative. The ability to persevere will enable one's passion to be sustained and will give them ample time to succeed. Patience is the foundation of success. For example, athletic pursuits are a great example of how you need to temper your enthusiasm by practicing patience. To be a good tennis player, one must be engaged and focused on their opponent. A winning shot is not something that can be achieved at any time. A tennis player must prepare and be in a position where they can hit a winning shot. It requires patience, as well as waiting for the opponent to make mistakes. It will not be in your interest to be impatient and make your opponent's mistakes.

Living in the moment is part of maintaining your enthusiasm. It is important to feel content and enlightenment. Successful people often strive for the best, but there are times when they are most happy living in the moment. Even though many successful people work tirelessly for long periods of the day, it is not possible to do so forever. Exercising themselves in professional pursuits will reduce enthusiasm. They need to be able to relax and take time for simple pleasures.

Chapter 4: Prepare To Facing Obstacles

Obstacles may appear in many forms. Some can be dealt directly and easily, while others may present themselves unexpectedly or bring new challenges. You can overcome them quickly by understanding their durations and anticipating what they will bring.

Obstacles in our personal lives are often the most difficult to conquer once we are conscious of them. If these obstacles are not faced and dealt with, they can create barriers to success. Emotional fears and negative thinking patterns can hinder your ability to make effective decisions. This awareness is not enough to solve the problem. These personal obstacles can be difficult because people sometimes have a conscious of these aspects but still believe they are more important than other people or that others should take into consideration those parts of their personality. For those who want to achieve success, it will take less effort to manage oneself and more to help others adapt to an aggressive personality. Another kind of personal difficulty is something that we transfer to our professional life from frustration or inability. Although romantic frustrations may not be pleasant, it's not something one should expect to see their colleagues in the professional world help solve.

Interpersonal barriers are people around people they interact with on a daily basis. Individuals may have to deal with challenges from their families, coworkers, peers in a church or another social group. Minor differences can easily get exaggerated. People are naturally different because of a variety of reasons. All people have a unique combination of personality traits. Although not everyone is perfect for every person, it's important to be open-minded and accept that. Communicating with new people will make it easier. This is a critical step. Many things can be overlooked when you're getting to know your new office colleague. If you don't use your best judgment, there are chances of miscommunications. For maintaining good relationships, or minimising damage to those who have suffered from strained relationships, it is important to communicate clearly. Understanding that not every aspect of someone else's behavior can be controlled will reduce frustration in dealing with people who are doing things differently.

Unexpected events happen to everyone at some time in their lives. It is possible for the "best-laid plan of mice or men" to be totally turned upside down, and it can happen for a variety of reasons. Someone can become unable or stifled by the unexpected death of a close family member. Unexpected circumstances can cause long-standing relationships to dissolve. There are many factors that can impact our ability to achieve the success we seek. It does not mean that your plans are ruined and all hope is lost. While it may be necessary for us to redefine success, we shouldn't dismiss it as a possibility.

Chapter 5: The Value Of Creative Thinking

Creativity is widely considered to be a crucial skill for future success as well as future generations. Amazingly, although all people are born with the ability of creating new things and dreaming, this ability is gradually lost. This is one challenge that the present generation faces. Some of the innovations that can boost creativity include new approaches to education and exposures in different cultures. Creativity, it is likely, was born from the need to react to new opportunities or change conditions in our ancestral environment.

Creativeness is a valuable social asset that spans all sectors of society, from the arts through to industrialization. This is important as new problems are constantly emerging that will require original solutions in a changing and increasingly complex world. To solve problems and adapt to a changing world, you need creativity. It promotes job creation, economic growth and innovative solutions to social problems. It maximizes the individual's potential by increasing confidence and decreasing stress levels as the environment becomes more complex. We can see the benefits of creativity when we compare the rise in global problems to those that were observed during its decline. The development of creative talents in children is crucial to solving problems in society and life. Young professionals who interact with foreign students or study abroad can gain a new perspective and be able to solve familiar problems. A lot of common problems can be solved if there is more opportunity for people to share their ideas.

Chapter 6: Patterns And Habits For Successful People

You must eat and digest food for thought. A person's potential brainpower is only possible if they spend enough time thinking about the various challenges and solutions rather than avoiding them. It is possible to become too focused in situations where it is impossible to separate yourself from other events or issues. If the mineral is used in fishing lures, or other recreational products, then it makes sense to become familiar with the politics and localities where tungsten is extracted. It is important to expand our interests beyond the local and regional news.

Aim for an early morning start. People who are awake early in the morning are more productive. This allows you to multitask in a world that is too short. You may be able wash laundry, get in a news segment, or cook a nutritious meal by getting up early.

Arriving at an office or other professional setting, the wheels begin to turn.

Live a healthy lifestyle. Cardiovascular exercise will help you maintain a healthy lifestyle. If you don't do it already, try to improve your eating habits and eat more healthy foods. Healthy eating increases mental sharpness, productivity and energy. This is one such habit that is foundational to success. This can come together with many other factors that have been discussed and create problems. It can become more complicated when it is combined with other factors like personality conflicts.

Do not accumulate too much. Get rid of all junk and don't allow yourself to get into a hoarding cycle. You should take stock of your possessions. Take note of what you don't need. High-quality items are more durable and better suited to your needs. This will increase organization and reduce time spent trying keep non-essential items from piling up. A reasonable level of organization is essential in every aspect of your life, from the mailbox to your inbox. Only save or keep what is necessary and throw out the rest. A better mental state and a simpler life can be achieved by reducing clutter.

People who are successful plan for the future. They must create a strategy. It's a means to hold them accountable at a specific point in their lives. They can see what is and what isn't working for them and learn how to improve their chances of success. Young professionals who want to start a business and have a family need to plan and develop a strategy. It can be more difficult to manage both in today's modern world, because children don't become farmhands when they are old enough. Children have become liabilities, and essentially they are assets now. Even if parents have the best of fortunes, there are still costs associated with raising children. Some professionals are more suitable for child-rearing. This is something that you should think about for anyone just starting a family.

Focus on the important activities and people you need to succeed. In order to achieve their goals, successful people have mastered the art of eliminating distractions. This results in more time being used to serve others, and a greater focus on people and things which will make the most difference. A few hours per day is all that is required for someone to leave their job. But they are able to use this time productively as a promotional period. You might find many people interested in engaging them. However, they must be selective with who they devote their time and attention. It can be hard to say no sometimes, but people who are successful have the ability and discretion to decide when something or someone is not worth them their time.

It is important to know when to live in each moment. Your life will be nothing more than a perpetual pursuit of a distant goal. This will lead to insufficient contentment. Be content with the present. There are things that you cannot get back. Admire the progress you see in your new employee. Give them a few moments to stop and take in their surroundings. It is better to celebrate small successes along the journey than do a big celebration after all the big deals have been completed. You don't want to miss another weekend away with your family while you are distracted by the trivialities of your professional lives. Allow yourself to enjoy that moment in your private life and return home on Sunday evening with a renewed sense of purpose.

Be open to personal development and growth that will help with dealing with any unexpected events along the way to your success. Your life is constantly changing. You need to learn more about the world and your own limitations. It is important to stay up-to-date by taking part in conferences and trainings. Successful people embrace change. They embrace the opportunity for growth and development that will enable them to adapt to changing times and even embrace these changes. If you want to achieve the highest level of success in any profession, it is important that you are ready to learn new communication technologies.

Step outside your comfort zone. Do not be afraid to embrace change. Accept a small amount of risk, as moving forward will require you to take a chance. You can't gain much from a decision which completely lacks risk. There is a data processing business that employs a new approach that is unknown but has been praised by their business partners. While this may not be the best approach based on past experiences, it's worth the risk.

Chapter 7: Knowing When To Make A Change Is Crucial

For one simple reason, change is essential for any organization: it's coming. You must be able adapt to change. This is a vital component. Successive businesses embrace change, not resist it. Refusing to do this will result in a lower level of competitiveness and a reduced ability to meet the demands for valued customers. Change is the only way to go if you are unable to adapt.

Changes in professional environments can be caused by many factors. These include the following:

Technological advancement is one of the most significant factors in change. It is something that most successful people know before others. It's incredible to see the progress technology has made over the last century. From landline phones with annoying background noise to iPhones, Android models have made it possible to communicate more effectively with others.

Automation advancements are another great driver of innovation in production efforts. It is those who adopt these changes quickly that reap the greatest benefits.

Time changes the customer's needs. With the rapid advancements in phone technology, think about the example I gave. Can a company survive if they only offer landline phone service? Delivery systems, and the communication technology that keeps drivers and dispatchers connected to each other will change as customer volume grows. It is necessary to enable drivers be able to deliver products to their customers in an efficient manner. An excellent example is the natural gas company that delivers to residential customers. If drivers were to randomly pick customers from a list rather than coordinate with dispatchers, fuel would be wasted and revenue lost. This strategy won't work long and the company might soon find themselves in the rearview.

Economic trends, good and bad, have an impact on the economy. This means that there must be change. Successful people will learn to take on the challenges of change. Due to the possibility of losing income or staff, the challenges associated with a declining economic trend may be more difficult. It's far easier to respond to the needs of an economic rebound because the chance to do more brings with it more enjoyable challenges that will be readily accepted by those who want to rise to the top. Other responsibilities or skills are always more pleasurable and easier to handle than reduced wages and decreased work opportunities. For professionals in real estate, it is important to be able predict large economic changes in order to reduce losses and invest in properties that will make the most profit in the future. In an economic downturn, people may prefer to rent apartments or properties. It is the reverse when economic conditions are bad and it becomes harder to get acceptable mortgage rates.

Any opportunity for growth must be taken seriously. You will experience all levels, though initially it will be difficult. These changes don't disrupt daily routines, but can introduce new challenges. You may be tempted to grumble when you are confronted by the need to learn another software program, or to move to a larger location for meetings. However, these are the easiest changes to accept. When there is a growth possibility, it is much easier for people to accept the changes. Being settled into a routine makes us feel comfortable and more relaxed. Growing is about moving from a routine to a new environment. Every new thing requires either a learning curve, or an adjustment period. There may not be an option. If growth isn't possible in an established organization it may not be capable of meeting some aspect customer demand. Inevitably, other organizations may rise up to take that demand.

Our society is more open to social change. Parents desire to stay home with their children in the early years. This is preferable to losing valuable experiences and time. Individuals who accept job opportunities in culturally rich areas where their professional peers have different views and values than their own will find success. They also enjoy the opportunity to learn from others. Many people are working later in life for various reasons. This presents an opportunity to optimize their experience. It can also lead to a decrease of productivity. Businesses and professional environments have taken a stand to be agents of positive change rather that being seen as merely targets. Incorporating social innovations into business can provide a great return on your investment. This attracts new customers, and opens up new markets. This creates a new identity that allows for innovative outreach. This is the kind if change that can attract people from many backgrounds to help bring new ideas and innovations to the marketplace.

Is EVERYTHING IN LIFE A COMPETITION??

D

You can read a lot about the beginnings of life. A multitude of microscopic and tiny sperm swim to fertilize the egg as quickly as they can. Only the one that fertilizes the egg and wins is the one that can create a new life. The millions of other potential sperms around are literally going extinct. In many ways, life begins with winning our greatest competition - to keep it that way.

Because a baby isn't yet aware, the competition continues. Parents will share the interest of their children if they have siblings. A human baby's competitive nature is quite limited. But what about animals living in nature? Many animals must struggle in early life to survive.

When babies are born, they learn how and when to win. A motivated student is determined to get the best grade in a competition against peers. There could be fierce competition to get into the right high-school or university.

As we grow older, we face more challenges. It may begin as a simple bet between two close friends about who can get a higher mark or be first to receive a date for an upcoming event. But, it becomes more serious as you get older.

Who is awarded a scholarship to attend an elite school or who gets admitted? Which is more important: the girl you are choosing or the way you look? Which friend in your group will be the first to marry you?

The real contest begins when we are a youth looking for a job as a student or part-time worker. We want to show and be valued our best abilities. You must convince someone or a group that the best choice is for them. I want her to be my recruiter. I want.' There are many candidates who would be qualified for a position. Sometimes, hundreds of people will apply for the same job.

We don't have to be the best, even if we land a job. Every day we must struggle and work hard in order to succeed in the real world. When we think we have it all, things can quickly fall apart. We might have to restart contest in order to find next task. I know I shouldn't let my guard drop and I may be in line to win the next competition.

I think that only a few things are given to us in this life. This isn't about hard work. This is about working hard and trying your best. Think of someone who died fighting cancer. Sometimes, life itself can be a challenge.

Where only the strongest live, competition is an essential part our planet's existence. This statute defines the entire creation theory of Darwin, and the fundamental principle for corporate practice. Competition is at the heart of all activities and interviews. Both good, and bad. Both good and evil?

On one hand competition is certainly the driving factor behind growth. Because even the spermcell entering the ovum comes from competition, it is an important factor in determining the human life. It is the most important driving force in industry, economy, and makes it difficult for companies to make more profit. It encourages students to pursue higher education and increases their chances of winning scholarships. Sportsmen enjoy the rivalry, which brings both spectators as well as athletes great joy at sporting events.

However, there is no guarantee that rivalry will always be a good thing. First, the person must have a competitor to be successful. Because each person is unique and has their own value, it's impossible to say no. The process of creating something is often hampered by competition.

Negative competition is when you compete so well that you want to win at any cost to the other person/people involved. The only way to achieve success is through failure. In our youth, we were taught that winning is good. Losing is bad. Negative rivalry is a zero-sum sport. It involves feeling greater than others or lower than others based upon their results or accomplishments. Competitive rivalry among internal teams can lower morale, decrease psychological stability, and negatively affect culture.

Positive competition is when we are able to perform at our best for ourselves and all involved. We are driven to succeed and feel inspired to reach our full potential. We are dedicated. Positive performances are good for everyone. Naturally, our competitors can either win or lose. The outcome of a competition can have a huge and significant impact. When we compete in constructive ways, we don't want other people to struggle and lose. We recognize that we aren't "good" or "bad" and that the outcome of a competition does not determine our worth as human beings. Positive competition is about grace, progress and the next stage for us and our teams.

Exercise is a great example. The best way to develop is to work with someone you trust. Let's suppose you and I agree to work together each day. We choose a few sports like running, cycling and tennis to do a couple times per week. Let's say that we wanted to make it more entertaining by having some competition. I would love to know how to run faster and cycle farther than you, and also how to beat you on tennis if we ever had to compete. Sometimes I feel stressed when I do a lot of exercise before work, and I might be unhappy or frustrated afterward depending on how that day was. If I set out to "win", but felt defensive, jealous, angry, or frustrated when "lost," then I might be inclined to taunt your partner. It is possible to still win tennis if you do the same things but in a constructive, collaborative manner. We wouldn't waste our time or add too much meaning to tests. Instead, it would be better for us to agree on a better training program and to motivate each other by pushing our boundaries.

It is important for you to put your focus on the competition in a team environment. We all have the ability to compete in both a positive and negative way. The better we are at recognizing our own and others' competitive impulses the more we can deal with them when they arise. Champion teams thrive when they harness their positive energy for collective growth and success. It will be easier for everyone to stand out if there is a healthy competition.

My view is that competition can be contradictory but it is also inevitable. It can be very useful in some cases. Culture can still be problematic as it is the only universal law of life. It starts with the destruction of the human soul and ends at a low, cultural level.

SET YOURSELF APART FROM THE COMPETITION

W

Why do you think you should try to fit in when it is your natural talent to stand out from the crowd? To differentiate yourself in business, your approach must be different. Achieving excellence in your career does not require exceptional skills. It requires hard work, determination, and a sense for direction. Do you want your brand to stand out? Here are six tips to help you distinguish yourself from the competition.

Find Your Edge: Everyone has strengths and weaknesses at work. You might be extremely organized, great at PowerPoint lectures, or an author. Whatever your strengths may be, make sure you focus and make the best of it all. These activities will be appreciated at work. Doing so will help you build a professional brand. It is a great idea to have some experience in specific fields that will help you advance in your company.

Have clear goals. Many talented people work with no direction. Be one of them. Don't be like them! Your goals should be clear. When you establish clear goals, you will be able to set a course for achieving them. This can help motivate you to make the most of your ambitions. Without goals, research may not be as successful. However there may not be enough direction and improvement. Set goals and you will be able do more for your individual accomplishments. You will also be able show leadership qualities that make you stand out among the crowd.

Do your best to dedicate yourself to your job - Although it is hard to believe, there are many people who will be happy to do as little work as possible and choose to spend their time on Facebook or working. Unfortunately, in the long term it isn't very successful. I'm not saying you should work every single day. It can be a great idea to take time off. It is crucial to focus on the task at hand while you work. Don't waste any time or lose your concentration. Don't lose your time. You will be amazed at the efficiency of your work if all you do is work hard and complete tasks in the most efficient way possible. Engagement is not only appreciated by employers and rewarded; it can lead to increased productivity, a greater sense for achievement and other positive side effects.

Be transparent - It is crucial to be transparent in your business. This will help you build credibility as well as confidence. What does it really mean to be transparent. This helps you be transparent about your work goals, objectives, purpose and responsibilities. Being honest about your goals and accomplishments will open up communication lines that can create opportunities. You are open to collaboration with others, not just for or against them.

Strengthen Your Weaknesses. Although it is important for your strengths to be improved, it also makes sense to recognize and address your weaknesses. Take, for example, your writing abilities. Do you know what you can say? Even if it is not your dream to be an author or a communicator, this ability must still be acquired. Learn to strengthen your limitations and improve your work.

Learn from Every Experience - Learning from all experiences is the key to standing out. Education can help you to break down barriers at work and make yourself more capable, independent, and ready for the future. Take the good and the ugly out of every experience. The best experiences will help you to learn and remember your strengths. You should not overlook your mistakes and negative experiences. They can teach you how to do things differently the next time. You will make an impact on the world and be different from those who are unwilling to accept failures and move forward.

Plan to Maximize Success - Create a plan. The old saying "Plan your work and make your plans" is well-known. When you are creating and building this program, why don't you set a goal that will ensure your best achievement? If you're willing to put in all the effort and money necessary to achieve your goals, then you can be confident that you will get what you want. Your life may be filled with happiness and fulfillment, or it could align with your values. If you place your plan at an appropriate altitude, you might find the time and happiness you are looking for.

Crystal-Clear Clarity-- It is very easy to lose track of what is most important in this "hyperattention era." You will have experienced it yourself. It happened when you were clear, concise, and centered. Perhaps you did it when you were 30 mins late getting ready for work. In record time, you were able to focus on opening the door. How many times have you managed to deliver a presentation or complete a mission in a relatively short time frame? Have you found it easy to get focused on the immediate task and eliminated distractions? You can achieve great clarity and laser focus by having this level of clarity. This will limit your personal development and hinder your business success.

Write down your goals. Your body will not be able to move there if it doesn't know what goal to aim for. How would you decide what you want for the long-term as well as the short-term goals? Which are your top 3 financial goals, long-term as well as short-term. If you are an entrepreneur it is essential that you have established business objectives. What are your career priorities for a professional? It is important that you have family priorities and performance objectives. You also need written guidance for any other issues. You now have the tools to make decisions about what you do each day and week. Make sure you have at least three steps to reach your goals to ensure that you're moving in the right directions.

Give your time and effort - Most everyone involved in a gaming game wants more and knows that he will need to make changes in his personal and business lives. These changes can take time and effort. You have made thousands of little changes to get to where your are today. The sooner you recognize the changes in life and take action, the better your outcome. Even if someone says "Result X" will take you two years, don't get mad. It won't take two years to get there! Would you prefer to be exactly the same place you are now in 20 years?

Get the Right Things in Your Life. With the power and attraction, you can achieve more in less space, be more energetic, courageous, affectionate, and make money. It is important that you understand how to get the good things you want. You can change your outlook, attitude, home, career, and behaviour to attract others. Attraction occurs when you make improvements in your personal foundation. It becomes a way to live. How you think can influence your behavior, thoughts, and performance. It can be amazing or very low depending on your thoughts and what results you are looking for.

Don't Make Yourself Accountable - Are you guilty of breaking your own promises? I know that I have. Your "word's" influence on an impartial third-party works exceptionally well. You'll make more use your obligations if you have someone to turn to each week. You see it all day, whether you are with your boss, spouse, or family. You can be nice to yourself, but not to the person responsible. Why should successful people require transparency? Can they not be sufficiently disciplined to just do it? With help, you may find ways to do things that you never would have imagined. How can you make an idea come to life? No matter whether you are creative or not, inspired or disorganized, the power of your word is unsurpassed in a coaching relationship.

Learn from your mistakes - Everybody makes mistakes, whether it's in business or in personal life. Accept them with open arms and learn from them. How can you say "dismisses less mistakes"? The old model of self learning is time-consuming, expensive, and very costly. Why should you have to make the same mistakes others made? It's a great thing to have a teacher. Someone who can see from the road and knows what's next is one of the many benefits. It will often be a blessing to have someone challenge your goals, aspirations, actions, and strategies. If you don't have any good answers to your questions then you might be about making the same mistake as someone else.

Stretch Your Boundaries to Grow as a Person. Every person has a natural desire for learning and development since childhood. Many people age out of learning and end up "walking the walk" when they reach adulthood. Learning and personal development are some of our most satisfying and rewarding experiences. I believe in "lifelong learning" and making use of the knowledge we all have. There are many books, seminars, and personal experiences that can make a difference in your life. People who love learning, want to progress and enjoy growing are the ones I work with. There are many reasons to use coaching for moving forward. But, development means change. Don't restrict yourself to what your did, or think that your limit is the only thing you did. The freedom and influence of your ability to go beyond preconceived borders as a human being is something that many people don't feel.

SUCCESSFUL AT YOUR WORK

W

Most people won't care what importance you give to your career. It's not just one thing that is "successful", it's many. This includes negotiations to raise or close a funding round for your startup. What is your performance at work?

To answer that question, you must first understand what success looks like in this context. If you're like most Americans your career is an important part in your life. There are many downsides to this job, but there are also plenty of upsides. What are some of the upsides? The upsides of close friends becoming close friends. Activities expected. A more purposeful feeling. You must take all these things into consideration in order to be more productive at your job.

Let's explore what success looks like from a scientific perspective and look at different methods to help you feel more fulfilled in your work place and personal life. In its simplest sense, quality is the attainment of an objective. To be more productive at your job, you have to determine what your goals are. Are you trying to increase productivity so that your family can be home in the early hours? Do you wish to take on a new role in an organization or change your work style?

Positive psychology science (research on how people succeed and live and thrive) has shown that people who feel a sense of their own abilities are the most successful. Research shows that those who are more successful at work find greater value in their jobs. It's something like 1+1= 3. Finding meaning in what you do will drive you to be better at your job. Furthermore, research shows that you could find meaning and purpose in your daily life. It sounds so good.

Let's put it this way: a successful job is one that inspires you and makes you happy at work. Is this an elevating goal? They're our favorites, we bet. You bet.

These tips can help you become a better professional in your field. This article presents 22 ways you can do the job well. Success in your career depends on your work ethic.

An employee is usually given a job outline, or a guide when they are hired. This describes your responsibilities, and the alignment with the organization's goals. If you are starting to work, you may have the opportunity to drastically change your job or make the effort required to receive regular paychecks.

Being internally inspired and in line with the organization's mission will enable you to develop strategies and other tactics that will allow your role to be successful. You can quickly skim through all the information in the table below, and then click on any tip for more details.

Exude Passion

Passion is without doubt the secret weapon to making your life more exciting, more rewarding, and fulfilling your dreams. Even though that may sound mysterious, most people believe that following one's dreams and achieving your goals are essential ingredients in life.

The dictionary defines "passion" as "a burning desire or intense passion for something." These words can be described as passionate, obsessed or fanatical. A key to success is the desire and passion to go.

For you to be at your best, you must think. People spend 80% of their time thinking negative and sabotaging any efforts to improve. The goal of this exercise is to be in control of yourself and to become an'should' thinker. It will help you better understand why your actions are what they are.

Everyone wants their job to be a passion. A job that is exciting and motivated by people who are responsible for a large task is what we want. People will move from one job to the next all their lives in search of a job that is fulfilling their passion. Passion is a motivating and optimistic force in the workplace. When someone is enthusiastic, everyone around them wants the same level. If you channel your enthusiasm well, passion can spread like wildfire.

It is possible for things to go badly if you don't manage this energy well. It is possible for leaders to have a negative impact on the energy and energy of their recipients if they are out of sync. Howard Dean in 2004 is an example of this. Dean, then the leading candidate in the Democratic nomination, was uncomfortably excited to a public that was just meeting him after a poll, looking red-faced and exaggerated. His cry became a Twitter hashtag, crushing all his dreams of the presidency.

It is more difficult than it seems to bring the right amount if energy. Leaders want to inspire, but how can they do this without appearing too high-minded? To maintain integrity and reality, it is important to have both honesty and the ability to see the truth. How can we make sure our resources are balanced appropriately? What amount of passion is right? These are just a few ways you can reach this spot.

It is essential to understand how others are inspired by our passions. Make the effort to see the first sights. To share a message or idea, it's important to first understand the context.

You can feel the energy of emotion. This is where a lot of change happens. What are you hoping others will feel when you speak your convictions? Understanding your message fully will help you to determine the best way to transmit this energy to others.

The situation you are in must match your passion. It gives the impression Dean Scream is overexcited. Too much is disconnection. A way to look at this is to put your strength on an 0-10 scale to calibrate you enthusiasm. Repeat the process to your audience. Now try to get an average energy level for both of them.

Here's one example of how this technique works: You try to convince your employee to accept a new project. You might get a 10, 5, or 5 (on the fence). You may feel more enthusiastic than you think. To communicate effectively with it, you need to reduce your energy to approximately 7. If you speak to her at a 10, you want to reduce your anger. Otherwise, you could disrupt the conversation.

The energy levels of the participants will differ if they are working in a group. You may ask your group to get a sense for the tenor. This is not science. However, some mathematics may be involved. Use your intuition and your intuition to calculate your space's energy. For example, if you see organizational language used constructively, this is a sign of dedication. Will you nod or sigh? Will you lean in? Or do they have the arms soft and the eyes moving freely?

In business, we are taught how to be stoic and convey authority and firmness. We still struggle to express what we actually feel. This status has one drawback: it means that you must share your love with others in order for them to feel your strength. Pay attention to your accent. Vanilla can sometimes be used to defame our claims. Use emotional terms to remove the fun from it. Ask them to feel what you are feeling.

Energy spreads, so the positive can also get distributed. People will share your enthusiasm if you are excited about anything. It's your job as a leader and to discover how much energy others should have for the task at hand. If you don't care, they won't necessarily have the resources to support your efforts.

You can use your strength to empower others. As you practice messages points, communication can also be energizing. We are encouraged by the heart as well as our heads. There is no reason not to include. The desire for him to continue to search and to discover his passion. It's why people often forget how long it took to complete a project.

Go Above and Beyond

It is vital to expand your horizons while learning. This means reading widely and learning about subjects you may not care about. It involves making use of free and affordable tools online and offline. Additionally, it will help you change how you learn, make you more employable, and engage you in lifelong learning.

You can read more if you take the time each day. Try to read the newspaper online and look at other articles to see a different perspective. A wide variety of genres is another way to expand your horizons. This can be especially helpful for those who read the same authors. It's not a good idea for you to force yourself into reading things that aren't interesting to you, but it is well worth the effort.

It is important to choose a subject that you are passionate about in order to improve your academic knowledge. For World War II knowledge, you may want to read more online documentaries. If you are struggling with certain topics, it is worth trying a new approach.

Open University offers students a wide variety of services. For example, online lessons are offered for no charge. iTunes

University lectures can also be downloaded, viewed, and listened to. OpenLearn Project and Open University offer free online courses that can lead into further training.

Try to learn a new way of learning by trying different methods. This can include writing a diary about your research, joining an online forum, and even keeping a list of the things you have learned. To show initiative, it is especially important to read about a subject before reading the English Alevel Review of Different Authors.

Learning how to write and memorize can make a big difference in your learning. To understand yourself better and identify your weaknesses in certain subjects is a great first step.

You'll develop greater critical thinking skills and be more comfortable dealing in unfamiliar areas. Even if all you do is use your wider interests for an interview, it can still make you stand out. You will be able to strengthen your key studies and stand out for employers by knowing more about many topics.

Do not be afraid to explore new areas.

If you think slightly ahead, plan as much as is possible. Look at ideas as alternatives to issues.

For routine work, you can develop resources for other workers. These are the processes that you can teach others. By creating process models and forms, you can simplify your workflow. These programs can be very useful in the formation process for new workers.

Learn something new every day. LinkedIn's survey revealed that workers who spend their time at work are 47% less likely of feeling depressed and 21% more likely of feeling self-assured, happy, and content. Three steps are necessary to ensure you're a successful lifelong learner.

Explore your curiosity cabinets - People who are naturally curious will seek out learning resources more easily. This helps them to stand out on the labor market. It is intelligence that gives you the most competitive edge in the industry. This allows you stay on top of your industry and helps you take on new challenges. Your curiosity can be cultivated by focusing on your interests and hobbies. You don't have to relate every new lesson to the workplace. No matter if you are reading a book or taking a class, learn new skills and get the benefit of others' experiences.

Set learning goals - There are some people who just want to be able to do everything. This drives them to constantly search for new information about the world. To make the most of your day, you need to do some lesson planning. To make sure your education is effective in your job, you must also be aware of your everyday work. The skills that you have on the job can make your life easier. Ask people who are interested and able to mimic the skills and use the tools, and get their feedback on successful strategies. This doesn't mean that Spanish can't be learned just for fun. Setting goals for your interests at some stage can be helpful. You can't learn everything every day. Keep track of the skills and subjects that interest you and find opportunities to help you achieve your goals.

Let's share what we know. It is true: "When one learns, two teach." Even if it is not your intention to teach, you can still learn better. Share your knowledge to strengthen knowledge. And people may be more eager than you thought to learn from them. A 2009 study called the 'protected Effect' showed that people will often learn more from those who are also teachers than if their primary goal is to learn. Perhaps this is because being an instructor requires a sense that you are responsible for learning. If you are looking to maximize your growth, be open to sharing and surround yourself by people who are also eager to learn.

In today's workplace, it doesn't matter if you are the smartest or the most clever person in the group. You can climb it if you are willing to learn. Begin to seek out learning opportunities each day.

You should be focusing on solutions, not more problems

All too often, when there is adversity in our lives, we focus on the negative. Only failure and hardship will bring us joy and not harm. It is crucial to keep this in mind.

If you want to make failure a benefit, and not just a chance to grow over the long term, then you must focus on how to solve the problem. People often allow their thoughts to turn to the negative. This causes them more to think about the problem than the solution.

Companies and individuals that are able to overcome enormous challenges and succeed in expanding their business are those who put more emphasis on solving problems than on creating new ones. For a quick example, look at Thomas Edison. Thomas Edison is a great example to show how important it can be to look forward, even after facing setbacks. Failure is never an end goal if this is what you do. Edison used every setback to get to where he wanted to be. This same mindset can be applied to our lives when tragedy strikes and we are faced with disappointment.

By taking the time and looking at your situation from a distance, while focusing on solutions, you will be able to recharge your mind. It will also help you focus on how you feel about failure. You will have a difficult life if your only goal is to do the easy thing. If you are willing to do the difficult things, life will be easier.

This holds true for everyone. It is easy for us to dwell on negative things in difficult situations. It's easier to stay focused on the important things in your life than on finding solutions. We need to be mindful of what we are trying to expand. If you focus on problems, you will run into more problems. We will get more options if our focus is on problems.

The next time that you feel like you are being defeated, faced with adversity or disappointment, think about the solutions. Not that you need to know everything. But if there is some way to solve the problem, write it down.

Our brains are activated by the idea of catching and putting ideas on paper. We are already thinking of solutions for our current challenges. Once we have a list that includes twenty- to thirty options, the next step will be to select the best option and begin to work out how to implement it. There are solutions, no matter how bad your situation may be. If you're patient enough, there will always be another way. This type of thinking will change everything about your business and the game.

Regular Self-analysis/Self-evaluation

Continuous improvement is only possible through self-assessment. It allows care settings to be focused on what they do, so that they know their strengths and can decide what they need to improve. Self-evaluation allows you to evaluate your service's strengths and weaknesses and identify areas for improvement. To determine if your service is able to make a positive impact on people's lives and achieve better results, you need to interact with, question, support, and think about people. It's an ongoing effort throughout the year that leads to continuous improvement, rather than a specific task to be performed for inspection.

It is important for you to see how your changes will lead to improvements in every aspect of your development journey. Self-assessment helps you to develop strategies that are specific and have clear goals. This will help improve the outcomes for everyone who uses your service. Continuous self-assessment helps you track progress and determine the impact of your actions on performance.

People who receive the service will benefit from self-assessment that focuses on performance. It's a way to find out what works well, what needs improvement and how to start your journey to improvement.

Success in self-assessment writing will lead to greater future rewards. This is because regular self assessment or searching for meaning will be a crucial part of your career development. A journal is essential for accurate self-assessment. It doesn't need to be written in handwriting; it can also digitally or electronically register.

It is an easy but powerful way to improve your personality, results, and personal relationships. Because it is important to focus and put your attention on your thoughts. This will help you learn more skills and boost self-confidence. Learn how to create a quality auto-assessment. It can help improve your self-understanding before you make important decisions that could change your life.

It is vital to understand that these factors play an integral part in the success and failure of some individuals. Not because they aren't good enough or lack certain qualities but because they lack the focus and self-discipline necessary to unlock their potential. So, to make the right life choices, you have got to be bold enough not only to question your inner world but also your ability and willingness for it.

Pay attention to these roadblocks as you learn more about how and why you measure your performance.

Emphasizing Perfection vs. Perfection vs.. Progress is more rapid when people or teams demand excellence. Acknowledge yourself for working towards your goals, even if it is not the end goal.

Prioritizing Performance over the Process: The majority of people consider performance progress. Only the most successful people can work hard to achieve success. Coach Wooden, the great coach, said that "Actual Success is measured with effort, and not results." Even if your efforts have not produced immediate results, keep in mind your dedication.

Emphasizing the Negative over the Positive: Wanting an in-depth analysis of what went wrong is perfectly normal. How many times have you stopped and thought about what went wrong on your way home? Concentrate on what you excel at instead of losing sight of the important things. Focusing on negative things can lead you to be more negative and produce less productive results. Focusing on the positive will encourage better behavior.

For personal or professional success, you do not need to be in a constant state if judgment. In reality, happiness and success are not mutually exclusive. Or, instead of focusing on the many things you need to measure, and how and when they should be measured, consider focusing on "one thing". For example: how motivated your team members are at work. Consider determining each day how inspirational you were to your team, and rating yourself according to a scale between 1-10.

Learn from your Mistakes

Effective judgment is built on experience. Experience is not the product of misjudgment. The following quote was made to several speakers. There are many variations. But it is important regardless of who said it.

Look at the recent success of your decision. What do you think your trust comes from?

Every day we make errors. Some of these mistakes don't change our lives and others can be fatal. Even if you make the effort to carefully consider your options and decide that you made the right choice, it doesn't always mean that you will get the desired outcome. There's always an opportunity to look back at your mistakes.

It is reasonable to think that people with this mindset would be able take mistakes as they arise, encourage change and help others to improve their skills. But instead we have a fear of the unknown that we can't control. We also try to avoid mistakes by trying to cover them up.

We see errors and not as foundations for solving problems. It prevents us taking responsibility for our own mistakes and makes it difficult to learn. Society teaches us that we should feel guilty and do our best to avoid making mistakes.

Let's examine the seven steps needed to learn from our mistakes and grow as individuals.

Recognize the Mistakes - Failures are your responsibility. Sometimes, people will blame others for their own mistakes and try to decrease their perceived interest in them. Accepting your mistakes doesn't need to be a disaster. You can just admit the fault and move on. You may lose your ability to accept your mistakes and make yourself look worse. Some may feel weak. Accepting your mistakes will help you gain respect from others. Accept full responsibility for any mistakes you make, no matter if they are your fault or not. While it's not easy, you can't change until the other person is accountable.

Take the time to show compassion for yourself. Instead, be compassionate with yourself and it will help you to remain focused on your goal. Research has shown empathy with your shortcomings can boost your motivation for achieving your goals. It's true that you won't get this far if your couch is full of TV. You won't get any benefit from ruminating. Consider the negative effects of what you did to waste your day. And, if it isn't affecting your growth, show compassion. What was your unmet desire to lie all day? Did you feel alone? Were you lonely? How can you take care yourself to prevent such things from happening again? A little kindness can help you make the most of any situation.

Ask Hard Questions to Yourself - It is important to reflect on your mistakes in order to succeed while also showing compassion. It is important to consider what went wrong, and how you can make it better. Look at the lessons that you have learned and how these lessons can be applied in other areas. Your thoughts will help you understand the situation. Writing down your thoughts will help you develop your logic in regards to a painful or needless experience. You will also be able to examine your mistakes and learn from them. There is nothing more frustrating than trying to correct a mistake you do not understand. It will likely only get worse.

Change your Mentality - People often forget to change their mindset. Make mistakes and look at your ultimate success not as a means to perfection but rather as an opportunity for growth. This will help you see your life from a larger perspective. This will help you to see the value in your failures, even if they aren't as significant. Let the loss go and remind yourself of your dream. Then you can keep going. It may take you seven minutes to be productive, but that is just a performance goal that focuses only on one ability you hope to improve over the course of your life. You make mistakes all the time. Try to learn from them and expand your perspective. Take a wider view and see the larger picture. Be open to learning from your mistakes and refocusing on the larger picture.

Create a Plan. If you're thinking about your future goals, make sure you have a plan to prevent you from making any mistakes. The program should be as comprehensive as you can, but it must also be flexible in execution. To prevent another running wound, I plan on spending at least two weeks lifting weights or cross-working. If my ankle begins to ache, I will be resting it two more days. This plan will ensure that I don't overdo things with my knee. If the pain persists after resting for a few more days, I might need flexibility in my plan. But I'll be able this to keep me on track with my last running destinations. If you are looking for an accountability partner, or an app that tracks your behaviors, there are two options. Also, different strategies may work for different people. A person can be inspired by an application, but another person might find it easier to just ignore the app.

It's not easy to screw up - Let's say you start running. Each morning at 5:30 am, the alarm will go off. Then you'll be able to fall asleep every morning. If you have the ambition to become an athlete, this is a terrible habit to make. Don't make excuses if results are what you desire. Do not depend on your inability to resist short cuts or instant gratification. Instead, you can increase your chances for success by making it difficult to fail. To increase your chances of success, you can either put your running clothes and running clothes out the night prior, or keep your water bottle chilled in the fridge for the morning. Preparedness will encourage you to get out the door after you have prepared for your morning run.

Teach other people: Teaching others has proven to be a powerful way to learn. Your mistakes can be used to validate your thinking. Share your mistakes with others to help them learn. This builds trust in others as well as consolidates the lessons learned.

While you cannot undo the mistakes you've made, there are ways you can respond. Recognize the fact that mistakes are inevitable and recognize that learning from them is part of our natural growth. Growth begins as soon as you admit to your error and then work on fixing it. These steps can help you to grow and learn from your errors. Your failures will be seen as opportunities for growth, not as failures.

How much horsepower do you bring to your job?

Can you deliver as much horsepower? How much work do you have to do in similar roles as others? What is the industry standard for your position of highest performers? What was the average work output of your industry one year ago? What do you think?

Try to be a top performer with your squad. A high-performance worker not only produces fast results but also makes sure that everything is done correctly and without errors. High-performance staff are the backbone and strength of any organization. Most staff work well overall, but every company employs top performers who perform above expectations and are crucial to the success of their business. Recent research found that 61% more jobs are held by top performers than those who are rated high by their managers.

How would you classify a top actor? These workers look beyond their job description each day, search for growth opportunities, use their skills well, and are capable of leading. Even top performers manage heat well, show love, and accept responsibility.

Managers reward talent at the top with harder jobs, greater responsibility, and higher salaries. Retention of top-level staff is essential for company growth. Managers should recognize and support top performers, and help them to grow and manage their company. High-ranking performers can feel disengaged or bored if they aren't valued and challenged.

Every job requires different skills and knowledge but high-performing workers all share some similarities. What makes an individual a person? It can be hard to identify an individual at the beginning of screening. They can still be a valuable employee once they've been working for the company, provided that they possess at least one of these eight attributes.

Passionate – People who are passionately involved in life and work exhibit a high level of enthusiasm. A motivated employee will be eager to learn new things and improve his job. Passionate workers have a passion for their work and feel great about it. Passionate workers are passionate about improving efficiency. They are also more open and happy with their job. Steve Jobs was passionate about providing an excellent employment experience when he hired new employees. He believed that motivated employees would recognize the purpose of the business, and worked to achieve the common goal.

Extra Mile: The additional mile can be specified but not required to do any more. Top performers will not sit and watch poor work and failures in their jobs. Employees who work hard and have a positive attitude will be able to perform at the highest level. They are the kind people who strive to do their best. These employees are the kind of people who regularly monitor the team's performance and offer support to other members. They also provide guidance in the event of a problem, as well as any other necessary steps to accomplish the job.

Takes Initiative – High performers take initiative and are able to work independently without external support and recognition. I would like to take on additional responsibilities and be challenged. The best performers are persistent in their career growth, make sure they learn the skills needed for their job well, and spend more time learning than other workers.

Open to Criticism. Top performers will seek the guidance and support of their superiors. You want to have complete information about your jobs so that you can track your job performance. High-performance employees control power and expertise within the company. You will interact regularly with your managers and supervisors in other departments. The feedback from the whole company can help you come up with innovative ideas. You are able decide when to follow, lead or get out from the way.

Dependable - The highest performing employees almost always work at a very high level. You only do what you promise. An efficient employee not only works on time but is also efficient and able apply corporate policies for each job. Only employees who are interested in improving their work performance and quality will be happier.

Empathy: Empathy can be defined as the ability or willingness to understand and respond to other peoples' emotions and experiences. Empathic people put themselves in the shoes of others and can understand their feelings and needs. Empathy can only be achieved if you are able to see beyond your own worries. Empathic people are flexible and open to changes in the thoughts and emotions of others. Empathy in the workplace involves respecting colleagues and bosses. We try our best to help others realize their limitations. We can handle last-minute needs and even face challenges.

Modest - High performance workers are modest and won't be praised for their achievements. Instead, they put aside their pride and let the work speak for itself. People who are humble, no mater how insignificant, will take on any job as they know that without them, there is no work. We all know our strengths and weaknesses. They don't fear asking for help. Because humble people are naturally able to share credit, it is easy for them to recognize that all efforts are a team effort, regardless how clearly individual. Humble workers contribute to a positive working environment by being kind and connected. You can reach professional personnel for assistance and suggestions.

Detail-Orlented – Details-oriented workers are more than just skilled at avoiding costly errors. These people are able to see subtleties that give businesses an edge over their competitors and provide insight into how they can improve the business's competitive position. They are the first people to realize there is no place like it and find what no one else can. Professional workers are proud of what they do and take care to complete the task correctly. A professional worker is someone who can look at the facts and is concerned about their consequences. They are also more likely to keep track of all details and double-check them to avoid costly errors. For example, Customer Paul used the word "consumeprofessional" in Texas Hard Money's feedback page for the definition of employee. It is crucial that the employee be consummated or as close to consummation as possible when they are working in scientific, medical, and financial capacities. It is important to provide information about the customer's Social Security number and bank account information.

There is an enormous gap between top performers of staff and others. High-performing employees work hard and are an integral part of the company's overall success. These top performers possess exceptional skills that differentiate them from their colleagues at the office. They take the initiative, engage in open discussion, achieve in a collaborative atmosphere, and are always looking for ways to improve.

Have Vision and an Imagination

If you want your dreams to come true, you need to think big. You can't keep all the things you want in your head and not find them. It's the foundation of your success. As you imagine, every goal that you can accomplish is possible. You just need to trust it. Act now. You can do it. Get it. That will make your dreams a reality. Here are the ways your creativity can help to achieve success.

Fantasy can be a motivator for accomplishing goals. You feel drawn to something you are passionate about. Glory, hunger, desire. This is how success comes about. Your imagination and emotions must be combined. Imagination is your practice space. It's where you express what you want. It allows you to eliminate errors and make mistakes, and it minimizes the time required to get things done.

Fantasy has a lot of things to do with reality. It shapes how we view the world and affects our hopes and actions. This means that you should think about what you want and not only what you don't.

Because you cannot make, build, or achieve anything without imagination, it is essential to have success. As you imagine a certain situation, object, or target day by day, your mental image of that thing will become more powerful. This is why you need to search for information on the target to discover its possibilities, and to make it happen.

Napoleon Hill said that there were two types of imaginative faculties. We link thoughts, ideas, or strategies from past experiences/information with the digital imagination and place them in new combinations to basically "create" something new from something existing. The synthetic imagination allows us the ability to process older information using new data, and combine these thoughts to create a more cohesive concept. When technology can't solve a problem our creative imagination provides a way to improve and develop it.

Through our creative imagination, we can communicate with new ideas. Although you may be able to see where you're coming from these new ideas and concepts, the creative imagination is completely new. A new idea, feeling and plan can bring you an "unexpected" moment of inspiration or a hunch. Only as quickly as our conscious brains function, can our imaginations be creative. We need to think clearly to get the most from our creative imagination.

Most likely, our creativity has become less active and well-respected for its ability to produce results. It is possible to revive and awaken our imaginations. This is similar to exercising a clean, underutilized body to make it more healthy.

Start with your imagination. Use the digital imagination. Make the most of your conscious thinking. Make a point to take some time to consider your future and start to prepare. Only by beginning to think and to prepare, we can wake up our imagination and help us find new ideas and connections. Reading is crucial for synthetic imagination. If our minds don't have new ideas, it is difficult to link old ideas with the new.

Utilizing your conscious thinking simply means that you apply logical and common-sense strategies to solve the problems of today. Some of the daily challenges we face can be easily overcome by common sense preparation, rational solution of problems, and rational solution of those problems. We can use our imagination to discover the missing pieces if our conscious minds are working at their maximum.

Remember that success begins with your thoughts. There are ideas within all of us that lie dormant, which can still be linked and combined by the synthetic imagination to form great concepts. We can benefit most from our imaginative imagination if we use technology and are aware of it. This will allow us to trust in our creative imagination and creativity.

A reasoning skill is something that every person can possess. This ability is very basic. Reason can be defined as "a basis or cause of certain convictions and actions, acts, facts, or events." With this, you consider how to draw a conclusion from the information you have provided, including your experience, situation and mp3s.

It is essential to use new knowledge to help you make decisions. This is vital because it will turn into a belief when you think and arrive at a conclusion. If you think straight, you'll be able to make informed decisions. If you think incorrectly, you'll make misguided assumptions.

Your results are the result of your convictions. If you have incorrect logic, this assumption will again be false. Your life is going to end if you believe the wrong thing. Your chances of success are slim. If you desire to succeed beyond your wildest fantasies, you must begin with logic correctly.

Learn from others

It is absurd for a young child to think that they will live a long life if others don't teach them anything. Our parents and other close friends, relatives and acquaintances are introduced from the moment that we are born. That continues throughout childhood with our teachers.

Society expects that adults continue learning. But, in a more specific way. The majority of society believes that our emotional development should not be discussed. Instead, we should solve problems for ourselves and keep it private. It is acceptable to remain adults and to acquire new skills to enhance our careers.

Such an approach to life wouldn't allow us to mature or change our lives in the right way. Life is learning, transformation and we need to be able, for the entirety of our lives, to do so without ridicule.

This should not be considered weakness if a human being wishes to grow and become more of a human being through seeking advice from more experienced people. This is the way we can both grow spiritually, and emotionally.

Many of us were inspired by our parents when we were younger and aspired to be like them. People who admire pop stars and soccer stars show boys wearing the shirt with their favorite players' names, rather than their own. Young girls may also imitate the styles and clothing of their favorite pop star women's hairstyles.

Adults find it strange that people whom we respect adopt a similar attitude. However, if that word doesn't seem too distressing to you, then it is very common for us as adults to admire other adults who possess something about us that we admire.

Their respect seems, more often than they are realized, to be due to the ideas they have in common as well as their perceptions of life in relation to how they dress and look. It is also possible to learn a lot about others. Even if we don't desire to be copied or cloned, we can still embrace and integrate our own values and beliefs into our lives.

Personal growth should not be taken lightly. Life learning should also to be taken seriously. The unresolved desire to learn and follow certain ideals, traditions, views, and ideas should never be dismissed. Do not let this go. Our personal development would also be impeded if we did not continue doing so.

Learning from others is a good thing. This doesn't mean that you should compromise with them on any little matter. Learning from others with whom we are not in agreement can be a great learning opportunity. What we learn about other people's opinions on everything is a confirmation of the convictions and ideals we hold.

Learning from other people allows us to be more mentally sharp, to make mistakes and to influence our decisions. You must be open and willing for others to teach you. They will bring many opportunities and new perspectives to your life. A lifelong learner can not only be an excellent instructor, but you will also learn from others' experiences. Many times, you will discover that you have much to share with those who want to learn from your experiences.

Volunteer for Lead Opportunities

Leadership skills are important for anyone looking to enhance their job. While you are at work, give yourself opportunities to manage small groups, plan activities, seminars, and deliver speeches. This will allow you to demonstrate your leadership skills.

Through these activities you can develop communication, teamwork or management skills. Look out for opportunities to participate in data collection or research. As such, you can still help to write reports even though the first draft is being written. Additionally, you can learn how budget planning works. Research, report writing and budgeting are all tools that will help you to be successful. Learn how to interpret financial statements to complete your toolbox.

Volunteering allows you to make connections with other people - The impact of volunteer work on the environment and society is one of the most recognizable benefits. Volunteering helps to strengthen your culture. The most important thing you can do to make an impact on the lives of others is to help them with the little things. You can make a difference by volunteering. It's a two-way process: you get as much benefit from it as your family. Give your volunteer time to your friends and network. This will help you improve your social skills. Some people find it easy to leave, while others stay. Volunteering can help you practice and improve social skills. You will also meet other people who share your interests. Once you've gained momentum, it is easier for you to make more friends and connections.

Volunteering is a great way to advance your career. Even if you don't expect to have a new career, volunteering can allow you to develop skills such communication, problem-solving teamwork, organization and project management. Once you have developed your skills through volunteering, you will likely be more relaxed at the office. Don't assume you already have the necessary skills, as volunteer work isn't paid. Many volunteer programs provide extensive training. No matter whether you volunteer at an emergency shelter for women, or are an experienced artist historian, you might become a counselor in crisis situations. Volunteering can allow you to leverage your existing skills, and help others. If you're a successful salesperson, you might be able to help increase awareness by being volunteer advocates for your favorite causes. Volunteering lets you try out a new job without any commitment. You also get a fresh perspective. Volunteering directly can be done in organizations that do the type of work you prefer. If you are interested to work in nursing, you may be able to volunteer at a hospital.

Practice Humility & Empathy

People don't like working with arrogant, boastful or proud men. A virtue essential to being modesty To improve your personality and focus on what you communicate, humility is essential.

The root of modesty lies within your awareness of yourself and your flaws. The idea that you can't possibly do it all or know it all is a shameful thought. It should be used to help people keep their abilities and efforts in sync. Recognize your weaknesses and accept that you are not perfect.

Empathy can be defined as putting oneself in another's shoes. It is possible to cultivate empathy by letting go your ego and seeing things through the eyes of others.

If you get stuck in a hold situation, please say "I'm sorry". Be open to admitting that you don't know the answer and then treating them as you would wish to be treated. You won't become someone who is just another person's doormat. Your limits and boundaries should be clearly understood and communicated. Always try to be kind. As much as possible, support others without asking for anything in return. Continue to plant positive seeds.

Do not gossip, do not waste others' time, keep your distance from unresolved grievances, try to be positive about others and respect their views.

Everybody needs a mentor to help them at work

Many people can comprehend the concept mentoring. You'll get 10 different answers. You may find similar topics among their responses. Mentorship can make a difference in your career's success. A mentor is someone who can provide sound career guidance and help you remain confident in your career. Consider these points when you are looking for a mentor in your career.

Contrary the popular belief that business professionals are always in control of every challenge they face, there is no way to know everything. For some of our hard-working hours, mentors can be a great help. Mentors can help you with issues such as coworker struggles, potential career opportunities and to enhance your professional abilities (communication, network, decision-making), offer strategic ideas and counsel you on career development and promotions.

A mentor is someone that will support you and your career. A mentor can serve as both a career coach or career promoter, helping us to develop our talents. A mentor can fill in the gaps you have in your career and help you grow.

A mentor is "a wise, trustworthy advisor or professor who is a leader sponsor or supportive." These words are just a fraction of what it means to be a mentor. These words represent trustworthiness, strength and assistance. All these qualities make a good mentor: someone you can confide in when you need help, another person who is important, someone you trust and who you can value their feedback and advice.

A mentor is someone who you can speak with without embarrassment. You will agree to your mentor that whatever topic or ridiculous idea you might have, this type conversation is perfectly acceptable and comfortable. Mentors should be available to offer support, guidance and time to help you succeed.

Your mentor should be someone from your field or someone who is closely associated with what you do. You should find someone to mentor you in your profession, regardless of whether it is a function area.

You can also serve as your mentor at different stages of your professional career. Although it is better to have a mentor with more experience and leadership than you, you don't need to be shy about looking for someone to be your mentor. Whatever level of experience or leadership your mentor may have, the most important thing about them is that they're someone you want to work with at any point in your career.

Mentoring is a rewarding experience. However, you need to recognize your own role as mentor. You are the mentor, and you must recognize your role as a mentee. To make your relationship successful and profitable, you must consider many factors. You must also give back your mentor in some manner. Create your own professional network and become a partner guide. Talk about your experience and offer advice. You can trust your mentor. Be an open listener and learner. Respect your mentor's suggestions and help.

It is vital to devote your time to mentors, to be there for them and to check in on a regular basis to maintain the mentoring relationship. It is important to recognize that this relationship does not benefit only you but also your mentor. Do not treat the relationship so that you do not reap all of its benefits. If you want to be an effective mentor, do your best at motivating and teaching your mentor.

Listen More than You Talk

How about I say that listening to other people is more important than talking to them? It is common for people to forget that they have two ears and only one mouth. Therefore, it is important to listen twice and talk twice as much. This way we can connect spiritually to others and not be driven egoistically by our need to communicate without listening.

The world could be a better place, if everyone listened to one another more. Communication is important. Everyone will communicate what they need and not hold it back. Conflicts are minimized, and people are educated.

Hearing from others is an art.

I will give you some tips that can help you improve your communication skills. A fluid dance can be described as excellent conversation. It is the tango of listening efficiently and communicating effectively.

You need to understand the difference between passive and active listening. When you listen actively, you should lean forward and listen to each word. If you listen 'passively', these words are often heard in both one and the other ear. Instead of being embraced by them, allow the sound of the word to wash you.

Listen to the Voice Tone. What emotions does it invoke in you? You can also assess the emotional state the speaker is evoking in you beyond the words they speak. Pay attention to the rhythm, tone and pitch of the speaker as it moves or changes. It's also possible to identify what is important and what isn't.

Hear The Sound Of The Language. Many of us use different vocabulary depending upon who we speak to and what our listeners hear.

Be aware of the Body Language of the Speaker, especially their face and hands. The non-verbal cues you give will indicate how you feel about what you are saying. It accounts for just 10-15% of contact (words). 85-90% of the remaining contact (mainly body language, not verbally).

Be alert about the signals - This often indicates interesting details, or short statements. Cues may contain statements like, "I need you to take note of two important steps." The first step is ...". Avoid the urge to respond, react or interact with other people. Your words don't flow easily if they aren't flowing freely because you have diverted your attention from the speaker. If you are prone to a premature explosion, either aloud or in your mind, it is possible to block contact.

Eliminate any disturbances both outside and inside. Refrain from talking about anything except what you hear. If you allow your mind to wander, your mind can become passive instead of active.

Although it is possible to "practice what you are doing", this does not guarantee that speaker's words will be retold. If you want to check the meaning of something you've spoken, use your native language to paraphrase and/or restart what was said to obtain proof or clarification.

Record your Call with Potential Customers or Event Planners. Please inform them at beginning of call that you're doing this. It's important that you ask yourself if it is something you are comfortable doing. This helps you to stay focused on the conversation. Listen to the callback to determine how long you spoke and how many words you said. Make sure you are clear in your answers. Have you answered their question?

Your listening skills will help everyone around you. It can take some time for you to become a good listener. A new habit takes approximately 21 days to form. It is important to be able to understand how you listen to others when they talk to you, or listen to them give a conversation. Listening to someone without thinking can help you settle any reactions or thoughts that might come to your mind. Listening to others may feel odd if you're not used to it.

Be self-driven and bounceback from setbacks

Write down your personal mission statement. It should be concise, clear, and concise. You should consider the problems that the team and the entire organization are currently facing.

Find out how to improve efficiency. What is possible? Use this to drive your internal self-drive. Do not expect to receive any personal benefits. Others should identify you with terms such as forward-thinking. As you try to improve your career and personal life, you'll face challenges.

Periods of anxiety can include low confidence, self-doubt or second thoughts and high fear. You must accept that the traffic jams are part and parcel of the journey. If you do fall, don't despair. Establish a reputation of persevering and finding solutions to problems. Employers will consider you a potential candidate if your behavior is consistent with the best interests of your client.

Even if not promoted, any major improvements that you make to your curriculum will boost your vitae. To improve your performance, you should seek out feedback frequently. Seek out feedback from colleagues and managers.

Speak up

It's common for people to refrain from expressing their opinions within a professional setting. Maybe they worry about how their image, or worse still, might impact their employment. Perhaps they are afraid of losing their valuable insights. Or maybe they believe it is futile to speak out- the knowledge won't make any difference to their business.

Remember this: even if you think your boat is great, it's important for your voice to be heard at work. It's not enough to have interesting opinions and information. It's worth taking the time to examine.

Keep your words and opinions to yourself. The team can take your feelings, beliefs, and emotions for granted. A positive way to be known is to speak up if you want a greater impact on your team, a better reputation, or to make a real difference in the lives of others. Talking to managers can be uncomfortable. It can be difficult for you to voice your opinions, and it is easy believe that it must be perfect to make it worthwhile. However, you can take a deep breath in and remember that it is totally worth your time-for yourself, your boss, or your entire company.

You can learn the most important lesson early on: how to defend yourself at your job (and in everyday life). It is unrealistic to expect anyone to think about your best interests. They know that they have a lot more than you do. Talking more is easier when you are aware and informed about the issues. Following the policies in the workplace can be a great start. Would you be interested in hearing more? Skip Beast. As a member of the site, you'll receive career advice and quest tips as well as insight into the work environment to help you become a better communicator.

In some cultures, speaking directly with someone is the norm. Subordinate leaders, while not likely to directly oppose you in certain cultures, may still be able to disagree with your ideas. For others, a simple critique can be the first step to a great discussion.

We recommend that you start with building trust in workers who try to talk to us. How can you do this in the most efficient way? Get good at your job. Good work will make you a leader. Leaders have faith that their workers will be successful because they display integrity in the work they do. There are cultural differences that can affect trust-building. It is common in Western countries to assume that a leader must at first be confident in their job. In Asian countries however, it is a tradition that he or she expects dependents to prove that they can trust him or her.

Conflict and anger will develop if you don't give input as quickly as possible. It is crucial to speak out sooner rather than later. Conflict and anger can escalate if you fail to give input in a timely manner. This could lead towards violent reactions.

Workers must manage their emotions. Workers should learn to be capable of taking control and to work with others. It is important to communicate your understanding of the complexity and value of your leader's job. It's generally good for cultures to speak up. Senior management should not allow workers speak without training their employees. The best businesses are open-minded and allow employees and managers to speak freely, without any problems.

Embrace Change

We avoid it, fear it and hate it often. Change is a dirty word. It is a disruptive force in our lives that changes the status quo. It takes us out of our comfort area. However, no matter what, we must accept that change is part of our lives.

It's today when the only change is happening and in certain industries and fields it takes control so easily that you can't see where it's going. Although you may dismiss or deny it, it isn't going anywhere. Accepting it is essential and learning how best to use it is even more.

You only have two options in today's world, where technology, customer demands, and business strategies are always changing. You will succeed if the adjustments are accepted as a fact. Once you are comfortable with it and have learned how to use, it will come in handy.

This was more than 20 years ago. The Internet came into being in 1997 along with the film and TV streaming service Netflix. This led to a mail-order subscription for DVDs. The demand from consumers was strong enough to make all sorts of businesses close and eventually disappear. It created a new medium which people accepted and changed the entire industry.

Even though companies are often the leaders in their respective markets, they can also be affected if they fail to adapt. Even so, the best improvements are difficult to accept for successful businesses. Kodak's was an example. Even though they had invented the digital camcorder, they were too busy with their film company to consider digitalization. Kodak and all her rivals weren't far behind and quickly became the leader in the field.

You can make a big change, no matter how you act or whether you think about it.

You say it's more difficult said than done. It's a daunting task dealing with change. Change doesn't satisfy us. Smaller companies are more manageable and flexible than large businesses so transition could be an important step. It's possible to make changes instead of reacting. Do not expect that you will be able make changes overnight. It can be difficult for your brain to work together, but here are some tips to make things easier.

Take into account possible changes in the business. This will make it easier to get used to your company's processes and procedures. Because you're so familiar, this is why. You know the basics of how it works. There's always room to improve. Get together with your colleagues to brainstorm. While you may not always want to make things better, it is important to be willing to do so. It is easy to become complacent. And then, the next thing you realize, you're no longer relevant. Stay informed, learn and constantly be curious about the latest developments in your industry. You never know when the next major breakthrough in your industry could be coming.

Keep it simple - Don't rush to get something new if you think it might be too difficult. If it scares or costs you too much, and is dangerous and thus stressful, you can talk to others about your goals and make small adjustments. It is possible to make small changes today that will lead you to your ultimate goal. However, don't wait for the climate to be destroyed by your rivals. Instead, take control if you feel stressed.

You must be open-minded and positive. It can be difficult for people to change their ways. We tend to be very protective of the status quo and take it seriously. Be cautious about any suggestions or improvements made by your employees. It will be seen as a challenge by your employees, which is quite normal. If you can clearly communicate your goal and the reasons why you want to change, your team will be more open. If you want to take things to the next level, it is important to show passion and a positive attitude. People can feel more positive when you are happy and relaxed. If you encourage others to contribute ideas and to make your work more meaningful, it will also increase the motivation for your work and improve your commitment.

Don't be afraid if you fail. It isn't a pleasant experience. Let's face truth, some plans might fail. That's the truth. Statistics aren't hard to believe. Does this mean that you shouldn't try new things, however? You should not. While it might not work, the plan could still launch you into the stars. While it may not work, it would be awesome if. Remember that even if it doesn't work, you can still learn valuable lessons. The failures of others can often be used to inspire new ideas. It's a worthwhile process, so don't rush into something that would negatively impact your business. It's important to remember that there are small steps.

Yes, change is inevitable. In today's world, it is even more obvious. 100 million people have used the telephone over 75 years. Facebook has become the most powerful social media platform for thousands of companies. It's easy to see how the Internet has revolutionized many industries.

Take the time to give feedback

Sustainable growth and improvement are dependent on feedback. You can get feedback from others about how you are doing, where you are failing, and where improvements need to occur.

It is a good idea for you to seek out suggestions proactively to help you improve. Feedback is an excellent opportunity to get honest feedback and provide insight.

Thank you so much for any feedback. Thank you. To make your feedback as useful as possible, you might also want to take the opportunity to research the matter and ask some insightful questions. We welcome feedback from all, but we must also receive it. Do not be negative. You should identify the bad behavior habits and show how they can change. You must get feedback quickly to ensure the greatest success. Feedback is less effective and more powerful if it isn't received promptly. When feedback is only provided after a long period of time.

However, if we wait too long for feedback to be received it negates its utility. Because of this, we are open-minded and are better able learn and retain information more quickly after an event. Fresh feedback is always the most efficient; impact-rich, valuable, and when an antenna mounts on the recipient the feedback is transmitted at the correct frequency.

Sensitive feedback should always be given privately. Don't make the receiver feel humiliated or embarrassed by the feedback. This could cause them to lose interest in the feedback. Positive feedback always comes from the path where there is least resistance. This usually comes in the form a reinforcement. It is important to get feedback from people who have experience and a positive attitude.

Get organized

A growing body research has shown a strong correlation between mental and emotional health. The evidence is vast and growing. It was especially clear that clutter is associated with depression. Many of these studies can lead directly to physical injuries, but organizational failure can, in general, have the same effects. This is the only question that remains after we realize that we need to coordinate for wellbeing.

You'll find more frustration and hunting if you're less prepared. An inability to plan can make it difficult for you to get on schedule or miss important deadlines. This can add stress to your life and rob you of your motivation. Your mental, emotional, or physical health can have profound effects.

The good news is you don't need to allow it to manage you. You can also take control of your business so that you don't waste a single day. It takes only a few minutes to build your own system for keeping track of the most important information and filtering out the rest. These guidelines will guide you to your own personalized productivity path.

To achieve your desired success, set realistic expectations. Stay focused on them. You should make them practical and motivating. They will help you stay focused on your goal.

It's important to keep a regular calendar. It's a good sign to let go if you feel like you are going back to sticky notes for making appointments by February.

You can set your priorities in the morning. It takes 20 minutes. Avoid your inbox, keep your schedule open and send your phone to voicemail. If this is something you struggle with, make a regular appointment to reserve it.

Prioritize the goals. Give your highest priority. How often will we be able to do the quick and simple tasks that are low-paying and put off the more complicated, high-paying work? Unfortunately, it never comes later!

Finish every day by putting aside time to tidy up. Send information to your colleagues, go through all of your work remaining and give it to them. Respond to voicemail messages and emails. File the things you want to keep and discard everything else. Finally, you can easily check your next-day appointments.

Clear your workspace. If your office or desk looks messy, it will be hard to keep track of your most important tasks. It takes only a few hours each week to organize all the paperwork necessary to cover every square inch of the earth. Do what you have to and put aside the rest. Though a stupefied desk is not an indicator of a brain dead, it won't help you be productive.

How do we invest in our organization? You can manage emergencies, disasters, and other things that you cannot control by being completely in control. You should be the best version of yourself, your staff, or your client.

How to Totot Your Own Horn and Not Be Obnoxious

All people want to make the most of their lives and their career. It is smart for you to add to your career with a bit of "showbiz" every now and again. You have accomplished a lot of "biz" through the steps described in this post. Now it is time to move on to the "show".

Focus on the things you've accomplished until you reach for your bell. It's a good idea keep a track of your accomplishments, so that you can document the key events or outcomes within a given time. For example, explaining your key accomplishments from week 1 or week 2 can take several weeks. You can also list accomplishments for the month of 1, 2, and 3. weekly. It is important to quantify the impact. Your accomplishments should be seen in the context of company performance.

Please choose an appropriate interval: email, one-week interval or provide an update to your manager on major achievements during the month. You can keep your employer up to date with your outstanding job by doing this. If your department/team meets frequently, and everyone discusses the important activities they are focusing upon for the week.

Performance reviews allow you to be spontaneous and scream your own praises. All your "toots", if they are valid, will be analyzed. Your entire automatic right to sound the alarm as loudly possible is yours. Another way to sound the trumpet is to engage in meetings, conferences and focus groups where workers can express their opinions.

Help others in times of trouble. Helping others is an appreciation of many. If you are a master user of MS Excel, then you might host brown bag discussions where you can share tips and tricks with others. If you are good at writing and proofreading let others know. It is slowly becoming known that you are a skilled writer and can help others.

You should update your CV often with information about what you are doing now. Keep your LinkedIn profile updated with your achievements. Ask colleagues and business associates for advice and include others if you need. Include any additional accomplishments, such a prize or appreciation certificate, in your profile. Still, be gracious and acknowledge compliments.

Unplug, Recharge

Attention! You may experience exhaustion and burnout if you push yourself too hard without allowing for downtime. Take time to unwind and refresh your mind and body while you are on vacation.

Before you go on holiday, you must meet your manager and partner to ensure continuity and to agree that your emails are not accessible and that you will not search them. You must remember to turn off your answering/voicemail system and to decide who will replace you in the absence. Make sure to unplug all social media channels during your holiday.

You can fly, visit friends and family, read a novel, ride, climb, camp or sleep anywhere you choose. You'll feel fulfilled if there is something you love to do. Surprisingly enough, there are many wonderful ideas and 'aha' moments that occur when you get away from high-pressure situations.

When you return from your vacation, you will be ready to inspire and offer new possibilities to your job. People are happier after a good holiday and are more likely to be successful.

Learn how you can deal with Ambiguity

Life's rich scenery is a intricately woven web of ups/downs. This dynamic and ever-changing world will bring with it more confusion and uncertainty. Despite the excitement that comes with change, some decisions can be overwhelming.

While you may think life would be dull or boring if it was predictable, there are moments in which I am sure that we all appreciate the predictability safety blanket. We can't always control what happens and we never know what lies ahead. The best thing is to be human, and to choose how you react.

Ambiguity causes uncertainty and can result in stress. It gives you the ability to feel in control over your life. However, we don't regulate our life. It is all about our mindset. It is impossible for anyone to believe that working is for life or illness. It is possible for circumstances to have an effect on your life. Even the most well-planned plans can make a huge difference in your life.

Ambiguity will be a hallmark in any company. It is essential that you are able to deal with it constructively. You can also stress out if you are uncertain. Therefore, creating strategies to help with anxiety is crucial for your health.

Here are some suggestions.

Manage The Inner Freak: Let's face it, everyone likes to be in control. We have to trust others under certain circumstances. In certain circumstances, such as when we discover we might lose our job, or are infected by a disease, we need to admit that we cannot simply wave a magic wand and ignore the reality. It may be necessary to place more emphasis on the trees than the forest in this instance. This will allow us to see the positive aspects of our lives and make it easier rather than obsessing over the larger picture. Focusing on things that are beyond our control can cause immense stress to the body.

Let The Whole Picture Go. In some cases, it is impossible to get all the information we need. You will never be able to know everything in a complex and uncertain world. Many times, only the experience you have can help you make the best decision.

Make a Decision Ambiguity can also lead to you not making the right decision. You shouldn't let this deter you. Even a bad decision is better than nothing.

Be agile - You will be able to adapt and change as you learn more. You will be able to hit a better target by looking through your eyes and fine-tuning how you navigate.

To be positive - A part of dealing successfully with confusion and uncertainty is believing that you can handle it. Confident people believe they can handle anything. They listen to others, offer help, and sometimes don't care about being wrong. They keep people from making errors and allow them to accept them. These qualities will help you be more flexible and responsive.

Avoid Gazing At A Crystal Ball. - Sometimes our worst enemy can be our fertile imagination. It can cause us to lose sight of the important things in life. If we don't matter in the real world, we will take the imaginary ball and "catastrophize". We are able to enjoy ourselves in a variety of "what is" Speculation is a way to create feelings and fears. Once we're in an intense vortex, anxiety can leave us behind. Sometimes you must get out of your situation and examine your responses and feelings. This will help you to calm down and create a more peaceful environment. It is impossible to predict the future. However, positive thoughts can help you become less anxious.

Learn Stress Relief Techniques. You'll feel stress while dealing with uncertainty. Over time, body stress can impact blood pressure and body sugar. It is essential to discover ways to alleviate tension during times uncertainty.

Tolerance. You can't notice what's going on if you are worrying about tomorrow. It is possible to let go of fear-driven thoughts and instead focus on the beauty, goodness and value of the moment. It is very important to practice consciousness. This is about being present in the present moment.

This technique may be most effective when faced with doubt and confusion.

Have an Entrepreneurial Mindset/Think Like an Entrepreneur

Learn how to function as an entrepreneur to make your career successful. The company's strength is its willingness, even at great risk, to make a dream come true.

Find new opportunities, be open to taking calculated risks, inspire others to see, maintain emotional control and calm during crises. These traits, plus confidence, crisis management skills, patience, and determination, are crucial for entrepreneurs.

The details are understood alongside the large image. There is no criticism and no bold choices are made. Humor and sweetness are used to communicate the hand, quality and performance are not valued, and the focus is on customer satisfaction.

If you want to be successful in your career, there are some key skills that can be used. You can learn to manage and be calm and still. If you are faced with a difficult decision, it is possible to fall asleep and look at it again the next day.

You can also show a laser focus on performance in everything that you do. It is possible to think like an entrepreneur and look for new ways of expanding your current role. Look for new tasks, identify areas that need skilled workers and position yourself accordingly.

Communicate this need and void with your boss and other senior executives in a thoughtful and straightforward manner. This will be a win-win scenario for both you as well as the company. You might be able to start a new career.

Another way to think like a entrepreneur is to see your current job as a long-term succession plan. Then, teach someone else how you do it.

You don't need to be the only one learning about the work. It's easier and more efficient to find a replacement when you need it.

Nurture Relationships/Relationship Building

Relationships form the heart of who we are personally and professionally. Your most important relationships will be worth the time and effort you put in, with either a parent, spouse or child, as well as with your boss, family or co-worker.

The benefits of good relationships go beyond the promotion of work. They also boost productivity. A strong relationship fosters trust and mutual respect. Relationships are not easy to keep. However, they are vital in our lives.

Diversifying your networks will help you build new connections. The next step in the process is to identify relevant people, including media and politicians from various organizations.

Do not be afraid to give your best. Only then will you be happy, able to provide support, and willing and able connect with others.

Strategically think about key relationships. Spend your time with your major clients, your most accomplished workers, and any other employees who can contribute more to the organization. These partnerships can yield both short- and long-term rewards. Avoid the temptation to engage in idle debates or ego growth.

Keep your eye on the social, business, and environmental environment of your area. Pay particular attention to your community's connections, loyalties, or networks. Recognize the norms of people's behaviour and their predilections. It will help you build a strong and productive network that supports your interests.

You should invest your time and brand money in key social causes - Find a group of people that share similar interests, goals, and beliefs. If you work with them, you can make them your strongest supporters and build relationships by working together to solve common social issues.

You should regularly trim, renew and restructure your network. This will help you to maintain important relationships with people in your company. Remove contacts that are no more useful. It is important to identify strategies for building new relationships, which will be essential for your company's future.

I am skeptical of all attempts to build friendships.

* There is no perfect relationship. Most businessmen are not able to build a large network. Make sure you carefully consider your relationships.

* Over-investing with relationships will distract from the work of your company's technical components. You can balance your time wisely between market responsiveness, new technologies and future corporate planning criteria.

Strong communication networks can help you stay in touch with the outside by eliminating new people and new ideas. Receive new information. Your network will be enhanced by new elements, new perspectives, and new experiences.

Your ability to design and implement a business solution that is perfect for you will soon be outweighed by the network's depth and breadth. These relationships can help you take risks without fear, to innovate continually, and to reverse losses. Your business is the nation and not the island. It can't be done on your own.

SOFTSKILLS TO HELP YOUR PROFESSIONAL CAREER

You have a credibility as the best programmer/editor/engineer, but if you don't fit well with others, it doesn't matter. The most important skills for employers or workers can't be taught or calculated in an office on paper. These skills are called soft abilities and are vital for your job search.

Soft skills are more subjective than hard skills and can be difficult to quantify. However, they can be proved and calculated. Soft skills can include interpretation, written and verbal communication, as well as leadership. Some examples include:

The Resource Management Society's evidence has shown that managers are much more interested in soft skill than strategies like math and reading awareness. Soft skills can make people's interactions more easy. Soft skills are necessary for building relationships and enabling people to be more visible. Although you can do everything you want to be successful, it is impossible to maximize your potential for success in your career. Learn more about your soft skills and the steps to take to make them yours.

Soft Skills For Your Career

1. Communication

Communication skills are among the most important soft talents an employee can possess. Communication skills are required in nearly every industry and work place. It's possible to learn and improve communication skills through the right training. Employees don't have to be shy. They can spend time learning effective communication skills. A public-speaking course is ideal for this situation. The strategies learned from talking to large crowds can be adaptable for daily interactions and most importantly, they create good faith in employees.

Why it is so important: Words and writing are key communication skills in the workplace. This sets the tone for how others perceive you. You will also be able to form relationships with colleagues. Communication skills increase your performance. It helps you set realistic expectations and achieve great results.

Why employers want it: When workers learn to communicate with others, they are more efficient. If you are able to clearly explain the whos, what when and whereabouts of a particular project, you will be highly sought after.

How to attain it: Toastmasters offers workshops for public speakers and is one way to improve communication and delivery skills.

2. Teamwork

Another important soft ability is the ability and willingness to work with others. However, not all workers are equally comfortable working in a group. Some may find it more relaxing to work together while others might have issues or prefer to work on their own. It is important to recognize these personality types before you start group training. A team should have a mix of personalities to make it cohesive. This ability can often be improved through team building exercises.

It is essential: Success in business does not depend on one person doing it all. A common goal is achieved when many people work together. All win when workers combine their skills.

Why employers want it: Team players desire to encourage employee retention and draw top talent. Additionally, it increases the efficiency of your job by allowing you to collaborate well with others.

How to do it: If you can, lend a helping hand to someone in need. It is also possible to take a friend with you on holiday to build friendship.

3. Adaptability

Why you need this: Sometimes events don't go as planned. This means that you must be able to find alternative solutions and not get stuck in your own way. Successful leaders know how be adaptable when faced with problems.

Why employers want it: Every workplace experiences high levels of change. Employers are looking for people who can adjust to changes in the marketplace and keep the company updated.

How to get it? Become an early adopter and supporter of the technology transition. It is essential that people are perceived as capable of taking on new challenges and being able to adapt technology without losing sight of what was true in the past. Ask your colleagues for information on training courses and see what they know.

4. Problem-solving

It is crucial for employees that they can think quickly, make quick decisions and solve simple issues. If employees lack the ability to solve simple problems (e.g. a copier not working), it is difficult for them to avoid office work. At least one person must have the ability to take responsibility and guide others in a crisis. These people are great candidates for management-level promotions.

You need it because: If you are unhappy, you can either complain about it or take action. The latter will make you aware. It will make your life easier if you are able to think on the feet.

Why employers seek it out: Nothing is a guarantee. Businesses rely on problem solving, particularly for top performers.

How to achieve it: Don't ask your boss questions, but a solution. You should sit down and plan your response to any situation that arises before you report it to your boss.

5. Critical observation

Why you should have it: If data isn't viewed correctly, it doesn't matter. Is there a trend emerging? What else should you look out for? A strategic observer is a great way to make a worker more productive.

Why employers care about it: Enterprises require creative thinkers, people who bring unique perspectives and practical approaches to help them succeed.

How to attain it: You need the ability to understand and use information to be an objective observer. One approach is to attempt to recognize patterns of behavior in the workplace. Do you see your boss reading the weekly sales note? What was her reaction to the negative news at the staff meetings? What is the best time to pose a question to your manager? By studying how people respond to the constant flow of information, you can better understand key aspects of business operations.

6. Conflict resolution

Why you need it It's part of our human nature. Your ability to solve problems and collaborate with colleagues is a key factor in your ability to retain and improve your work relationships with them.

Why employers want it This individual promotes a collaborative, healthy workplace.

How to do it: To resolve differences between workers, you must deal with them directly and in a sensible manner. Let everyone in a friendly environment of mediation, free from judgment, work together to solve their issues.

7. Leadership

You can inspire colleagues by believing in your vision and being clear about it.

Leadership skills will allow you to be recognized in a company and get promoted or pay bumps.

Why employers want it

How to attain it: Leadership doesn't necessarily mean people can do anything they want. Leadership makes sure others are motivated to reach their potential. This can be done by being an intern boss. It gives you the chance to lead, inspire, take charge, and make decisions.

This is why it is more important to have soft qualifications than ever.

Hard Skills Without Soft Skills - The technical skills required for most jobs aren't enough to be successful. Without the required interpersonal skills to negotiate and retain customers, even a market expert with great product knowledge and market knowledge, a seller will not be very successful. A business manager must have the ability to listen to staff and to think creatively. For all professions, at least some soft abilities are necessary to improve hard skills.

Soft Skills aren't hard to master – Hard skills are easy to learn. You can learn quickly and then you can grow and improve. Soft skills are less dependent on experience and knowledge, but they are closely tied to the person's personality. For wealth to be built, it takes effort, perseverance, and self-development. While your resume might be full of hard skills, your soft skills will help you stand out among other candidates with comparable experience.

Modern Workplaces Are Interpersonal. - You need to be able to listen, work with others, share ideas, and communicate with them. Good soft skills are critical to organizations in today's highly competitive work environment.

Customers Demand Soft skills - The digital market gives customers infinite options using technology like the Internet and smart phone. For these customers comfort and low prices are easily accessible. This is why the customer service aspect of a company's preference is so important. This is an important factor in determining the success of a business's ability and willingness to work with customers.

The Future Workforce will depend on the ability to develop soft skills - Artificial intelligence and automation intelligence will lead us to more jobs that require soft skill. Technology is making it easier to develop soft skills. Deloitte Access Economics' smart study found that soft skills will account for two-thirds in Australia's future employment. This phenomenon is eventually reflected worldwide.

You can see why developing soft skills is important in the workplace. You are now aware of your goals and looking for new ways to stand out in the workforce. Enter Monster is free today. You'll receive practical career advice, tips and other useful information directly to you inbox as a member. We offer everything from wage negotiation to lists of top employers that are hiring. We will help you learn how to put your talents to work.

HARD SKILLS AT THE MODERN WORKPLACE

H

The skills called ard are the skills you need to do a particular job's duties. Hard skills enable you to do the job easily. If you're an engineer for example, your hard work will involve math, calculations, as well as research. However, not all technical jobs require hard skills.

For personnel-oriented positions such as sales, skills include product knowledge, study interpretation, data mining, lead generation and customer information. These soft skills can help the engineer and salesman accomplish their tasks.

Types Of Hard Skills

There are several types of hard skills. The following fall into these categories:

People-oriented: Professions such a banking, project management and management all have certain systems and methods that guide how they conduct their duties. This includes the ability to comprehend schedules, project finances, filing systems and risk assessment strategies.

Research & Analysing - These skills are used to extract, analyze and develop knowledge. Translating, statistical analysis and transcription are some of the skills needed to generate particular ideas or solutions with data.

Manual Skilled Work - These are electrical, building and manufacturing as well as plumbing and woodwork.

Professional Services – These hard skills require intensive preparation and study. These skilled practitioners will train and specialize. You may also find them accredited or licensed to work as professionals in different institutions and companies. Accounting, legal work, dentistry, programming in computer programs, and engineering all count as professional hard skills.

Creative Hard Skills: These are skills used in creating the art form they desire, depending on their work and customer requirements.

The Resume Guide for Hard Skills

Computer/Information Technology Skills. Computerized work environments are the new workplace. Many processes in companies and work were already automated. It is anticipated that most job seekers today will have intermediate Microsoft Office, search and cloud computer skills. Recruiters expect applicants have a working understanding of related business technologies. They also require candidates to have data storage, management, presentation and presentation skills.

Communication is difficult - Communication might not be considered as a common skill. Based on the job requirements, some communication skills may be required. A communication job, for example, may require writing, talking, or selling the content. Your curriculum vitae should include the ability to design User Experience (UX), or speak foreign languages.

Agile Project Management - Project management is essential for modern workplaces. Agile project management includes teamwork, flexibility and cooperation.

Digital Marketing - The broad scope of digital marketing includes SEO optimization, content creation, assessing ROI (Return on Investment), email marketing and data mining. These profitable activities will distinguish the curriculum vitae.

Web/App Developer - This skill is well-suited for the 21stcentury. Apps that stream videos, navigate geographically, and locate nearby businesses are all examples of web/app development. The website or application can be used to perform banking, order food, show entertainment, and browse company catalogs.

Security control/Risk management: With the high rate of crime in Trinidad and Tobago and rising threat of malware and cybercrime, recruiters must value skills like risk assessment and firewall protection.

Make sure to include a section on your resume that demonstrates how much you've learned. It is a good idea to mention certifications and other specialized training courses in this section. This is a 'do NOT tell to me' society. Your resume must demonstrate that your skills are practical. Your ability to demonstrate your accomplishments must be clear in order to make it possible. Have you ever used your

SEO expertise to create 5,000 new online advertising campaigns?

You were instrumental in developing an app that would allow consumers transact and reduce wait times for cashiers. Discuss your work history and how you used your skills to get a job done, solve a challenge, or get a good result.

Recruiters may ask for examples to demonstrate your problem-solving skills. Sometimes you use your marketing skills and solve technical problems in your programming skills. Strong evidence is needed to support the requirements of recruiters.

Employers often want to know if you have a strong communication skill about anger customers, dissatisfied colleagues or disputes managers. You can also talk about the job description and how a particular scenario, or activity will be performed. If you are the nominee who is looking for his squad of men, the approach that you give will explain.

How to improve your workplace skills

Based on the hard skill level you wish to develop, it is important that you decide which approach is most effective.

Person Investment: Expert preparation, job services, or training can all be used to enhance technical, artistic and manual study abilities. To increase your abilities in the workplace, you can enroll in many government-funded programs. Training services can be offered by several organizations, including universities, training organizations, and business schools.

Practice makes perfect. Some skills, such as people-oriented hard skills, need to actually be honed in an effort to become better. An applicant can create content or design graphics to help them develop new strategies, improve their professionalism, and make their work more efficient.

Find a Mentor. Often, a mentor will help you gain a deep understanding and demonstrate the performance of a skill. Coaching can offer practical advice that you can use to help you learn quickly.

LEARN NEW SKILLS FOR YOUR CAREER DEVELOPMENT

W

Learning should not stop once one's college or school is finished. It should continue for as long and as our lives allow it. This applies equally to your work life. Learning is key to your career advancement due to the constantly changing demands in today's workplace.

Continuous education is vital for today's workplace. Today, technology, processes, as well as how we communicate, all play a major role in our communication. It is unlikely that you can do enough to refresh your knowledge. You are capable of staying on top of the latest technologies and developing your skills. Your employmentability will depend on it.

Employers must not only be able play their role but also have the ability to think strategically and resourcefully. These are people who work hard and take on projects.

Workplaces are so stressful today that workers have little to no time for personal development and skills growth. As new technologies develop, workers have more options for growth. To be ahead of your peers, it is crucial to increase your skills and learn new skills via the best career progression plan.

Here are five major reasons why it is important to acquire new skills in life.

More Career Opportunities. You will be more qualified for employment if you acquire new skills. Employers don't care about what degree you have or technical qualification. Employers care only about the skills you have to bring value to your business. These skills will allow you to get a great job even if it isn't college-level. You should continue to improve your skills and seek out new opportunities.

Make More Money. The world is becoming increasingly expensive. To be able to pay good money for the work that you do, you must have skills that are valuable. You pay more for work the higher your talents and the more exceptional you are. A beautiful house in a great location will inspire you to live well.

Changed social life - This will allow you to create new social networks and gain new skills. You have the chance to meet others with similar talents. This allows you to make more friends and enhance your social life. This could translate into more parties and gatherings with your friends. It's possible to find someone more than an acquaintance if your partner is not yet a romantic one.

More self-confidence - A person with a large knowledge base and expertise will feel more confident. Low self-esteem and confidence are rare signs of intelligence. You can achieve things that are difficult for the average person with more skills. This will help you feel good, and it will also increase your faith in reaching new heights.

Teach Others – Don't leave them behind with all your new skills. It is essential to show other people your talents and encourage a "paying it forward" mentality. People will find amazing opportunities to work and live better lives if they do this. The world would be better if more people were willing to share their talents. It would result in more people feeling confident and having the ability live.

As we mature and become more engaged in our lives it becomes more difficult for us to promise new skills. These six steps will help to get you back in the learning phase.

Get Mentally, Physically and Spiritually Invested in the Skill - Ask what you want to do with your lives. You must always ask why. Because you will only be able overcome any obstacles in your journey to your goal if your reason is strong (the emotional motivation to improve your self). Competencies do not discriminate. They are like an elephant who cannot be stopped. Although you may sometimes have a reason, you will still find yourself feeling guilty. Practically speaking, this means you have to channel your motives towards specific actions, not self-pity. Regular, weekly workouts are the best. Maybe you won't do it if your schedule doesn't allow it.

Make sure your reason does not stem from a lack talent. Talent can definitely help. It can make a big difference. It's not possible for everyone to be creative. Importantly, an "all-or nothing" game is not talent. However, this doesn't mean that talent can't make you do better at something. Make sure you don't lack the talent to make an impact or learn new skills. In terms of talent, it is prudent not to have double standards. Talent is overrated if it doesn't come with the ability to learn. Talent does not always outweigh hard work. The hard work you put in will make you stronger and more resilient. It doesn't matter if you don't have a talent. There is tremendous value. You can't understand the feeling of life if it doesn't feel like it. It is difficult. People who are good at something may not have a special perspective. If you have a unique view, you can always write a book.

Step out of Your Comfort Zone - You will need to restructure your work schedule to find new possibilities for yourself and build a better future. Being a master at something takes time. While you may be comfortable with your role, it is not a sign of a master. Get to know the main business areas and get to know the people in the organization. Be open to all possible perspectives and make a decision to focus on one. You can help a business unit achieve its goals in a more effective, efficient, and economical way.

Time is Expended - If time has been taken away from you, it must be efficiently managed. The longest time that your day will take. It's important to determine how you can make time to explore new possibilities and not interfere with your current work schedule. Every day is a learning opportunity. You'll feel motivated to continue your professional development if you are positive about it. You can learn a lot by developing habits in just a few short weeks. Be productive in your daily activities, but make sure to also take the time to learn and grow.

The Best Advice For Getting a Mentor or Coach is - I've tried many different strategies, tips, and suggestions when practicing and learning new skills. This is an excellent trend. To learn a new skill, get a mentor. You shouldn't go with anyone. Look for someone who can mentor you. Make sure you've learned the necessary skills to become a mentor. Importantly, look at your past experiences and make sure the coach has taught you the same thing as you have in the past.

Set realistic expectations for learning a new skill. There is nothing that will keep you from mastering new skills faster than major mistakes. If you have unrealistic expectations as to the speed at which you will learn a new skill, then you will fall behind your goals sooner than you think. I had unreal expectations when it came to coding. If you don't manage expectations well, the joy of learning new skills will quickly turn to disappointment. What are realistic expectations however? Nobody has the right answer. Experts in performance psychology have different reactions. We do have some guidelines and facts that can be used to determine the cost of new skills.

* It takes between 25 and 30 hours to master any skill. This is sufficient to guide and take you through the basics.

* The investment required to reach the global mastery level is approximately 10,000 hours. However, the time invested only reflects an output gap between 10-20%. Practice is the only prerequisite to mastery.

There are many other factors that influence your potential success. It is important to have talent, practice consistency and program structure reliability. However, you don't have to be an international master. It doesn't mean you have to act like a diplomat.

To reach strength enough, it takes somewhere between 25-10,000 hours. If you use the best learning strategies, you can reach 25 years more than 10,000.

* Every skill starts slow and is frustratingly difficult. After your first frustrations, fast learning acceleration happens. It is then

that you hit a plateau. From here it becomes harder and easier for you to get better. Problems with persistent incompetence or plateaus are when it comes skill acquisition. This is where your strength, endurance and determination are key.

These are important facts to keep in mind when managing standards. It's difficult and stressful to get started. Once you recognize how inept your current situation is, you will find that the first few hours spent on deliberate exercise are successful. The next five- to fifty hours are critical. If you have a plan and are willing to practice correctly, you'll make great progress. Be prepared to dedicate 25-50 hours to learning a new skill. Do the math. It takes 45 to 60 minutes each day, three days a weeks for three months. You will train. This is the time to invest in the foundations.

Be prepared to take chances. Even the smallest of risks can benefit you. Be willing to take risks, and not be afraid of taking chances. This will allow you to be open to new opportunities, ask questions, and complete tasks you have never completed. As you grow in your career, you will be able to take on new challenges and gain new skills.

Strategize Your Tasklist - Sometimes learning is a passion. But you won't be able to do everything you want in a single day. While you may have planned a well-planned day, it was too time-consuming to complete all of your missions. This may be because you didn't know how to properly schedule your day. Most people confuse execution planning with planning. Strategy is not just about doing a task. It involves making it more productive and less time-consuming. It's more than a plan. This can easily be accomplished by watching professionals in less time. Track and follow important people to improve your skills and help you strategize. This is a skill you can use to grow your career.

For every skill you are interested in learning, set specific goals. There are hundreds of online courses, coaches, books and other resources. This could seem intimidating. We can appear to do nothing in the middle of a series of choices. That is something you need to avoid. You need to avoid this. Avoiding the tyranny is to define in detail and comprehensively what level of know-how you wish to acquire. It is an excellent way to create practical value. Acquiring a new skill will ensure that you are always able to solve a problem. After mastering a specific skill, you can introduce a different one. This strategy cannot be confused. The biggest danger is getting overwhelmed and lost in the information overload.

Demand new work. Be ready to accept a lower salary in order to find new opportunities. You might need to develop new knowledge or learn new work before you are fully transferred to the new role. It is important that you are open to new, payitforward work to improve your career. Relying on resources is possible once you have the necessary skills and knowledge to lead a project beyond your normal area.

You can learn skills online by taking a short-term course. You should first look for the information you can learn. These are the days and times that you will be able enroll and begin to learn online with loads and lots of excellent material. You can learn new skills quickly and easily online.

Preliminary and Knowledge Planning - Once a goal has been established and the knowledge that you wish to gain, you will have enough time to conduct initial research and create a plan of action for your learning. The first is the research into the best options. You will find the best videos, books, online courses and coaches for all your skills if only you put in a little time to study. You'll find it difficult to choose what you want to study and how to access the best knowledge. The next step is to build your skills. An increase in ability is usually made up of several sub-skills. These are the core components of that ability. The first step is to divide all skills into small, practical sub-skills. Learning must be easy and not overwhelming. It is an aspect of life. This can be helpful in identifying the most pertinent competencies and allowing you to focus on them.

To succeed, create a supportive atmosphere. Strong environmental protection is essential. Acquiring a new skill is no exception. The environment must be set up so that you feel validated for your work. The best way of managing your life is not to be perfect. Let's suppose you are going to become unmotivated, lazy and ignorant at some time. In that situation, you will need support networks to help you get back on track. Here are some examples.

* For practice sessions, you can create a series reminders (on your mobile, laptop, or desktop)

* Get books.

* Use this tool to change your desktop wallpaper and remind you of the power of inspiration.

* Make it easier to access information and to improve skills learning.).

* Attend gatherings. Make new friends.

Reward yourself for every job you do.

* Work with a customer to help you master the skills. You must set realistic goals. Keep your commitments and deliver.

Don't let your self-discipline go without you. Your environment should be supportive. This is essential as it is half the formula for success.

Instant Implementation, Feedback System - You can read 100 swimming books and it is almost like taking a leap in the water. Although you are eager to learn, make a plan, and then put it into practice, it is essential to get the most out of your knowledge. This is how you know the most. You can avoid intellectual paralysis with a realistic project. The good news about this is that the majority skill sets deal with practical problems. This is a great sign that skills are in high demand. It's easy to keep your skills up with practical work and move into different projects. Practice your skills whenever possible. This is where you can gain real-world experience. Get feedback from others on the results of your research. Experts and trusted friends can provide additional advice and guidance on how to improve things.

Compliance with The Best Practices of Learning: When learning new knowledge, the exact same rules apply. But, the problem is that most best practices are not intuitive. We believe that we can pack learning sessions and repeat the same thing endlessly, then practice it in the exact same way. However, it isn't true. This approach is most ineffective.

The best ways to learn are:

* Chunking Strategy: Separate the learning content into manageable chunks (in this case, subskills).

* Concentrated concentration: Focus completely on the task at hand and avoid distractions. Concentrate your mind on learning.

* Take breaks. Take a quick break after a 45-60 minute session to increase your concentration.

* Spatial repetition: A 12 hour period for 5 days is much more realistic than 5 hours per day.

* Concentrate exercise. Do concentrated stretches, workouts, and stretches before you begin to work on one particular area.

* InterweavedPractice: In a single session you will use different concepts approaches and strategies. You can mix the practice, speed up or slow it down; perform assessments; practice different things; etc.

* Do not stay in your comfort zone. Do some things outside of your comfort zone. Always use your expertise to the fullest.

* The stage in which you master a particular chunk. When frustration is your only emotion, then you've achieved something. Use a chunk before you're bored.

* Rest. You must rest between sessions if you want to see improvements. There is no progress without rest. Learning knowledge and skills can change your brain. It takes time and rest.

List the Skills you Want To Master and Sort Them Correctly - Get a piece of paper and start to list the skills you wish to master. You can probably list 10 to 15 skills easily. They are difficult to master all at once. It's best to master two to three skills at a time in your spare hours, while you work. Next, you need to decide how you give priority your abilities. This can be achieved using many criteria.

* The main point of the skill is to be able to identify multiple categories. You can improve productivity, enjoy a hobby, increase your quality of life, or enhance your relationships skills and exercise. Learning new skills is a great way to increase your productivity. This is the goal.

* Supply/demand: In order to increase the market worth of your competencies, it is important to develop high demand skills while minimizing supply. These are the attributes that significantly increase your profits. Hobbys have a much lower market value.

* Talent: You don't need to waste your talents. This is a lesson in the Bible. Classify

your skills into the abilities that you are skilled at, neutral in, and talentless at.

* Your year-end goals and focus: Your capability training programme will be part your long-term targets. Learning special skills is a way to improve your job prospects or change your life.

* Current opportunities What will your company pay for you to learn your skills? A friend or a colleague who has learned something can be able to mentor. Is it possible to enter a job that is paid?

* You have resources: To learn skills, you need emotion, finances, and time. We have seen this before. Gaining more abilities is more difficult. It is important to evaluate your current level of expertise.

www.ingramcontent.com/pod-product-compliance
Lightning Source LLC
Chambersburg PA
CBHW050025130526
44590CB00042B/1907